NORTH-EASTERN BRANCH LINES

PAST AND PRESENT

Ken Hoole

Oxford Publishing Co.

Typesetting by:
Aquarius Typesetting Services, New Milton, Hants.

Printed in Great Britain by:
Biddles Ltd., Guildford, Surrey.

Published by:
Oxford Publishing Co.
Link House
West Street
POOLE, Dorset

Witton-le-Wear Station on the Wear Valley branch; a single storey version of an NER station design of the 1880s. The station was authorized in 1888, replacing an earlier station, but lost its passenger service in 1953 and has since been demolished. However, the line is still open to the cement works at Eastgate.

K. L. Taylor Collection

Contents

Foreword

This work is an attempt to provide a comprehensive picture of branch lines in North-Eastern England in the days of the North Eastern Railway, the London & North Eastern Railway, and British Railways. The book is divided into five sections:

Section One:
A look at every station on one particular branch, (Alnwick to Coldstream) when completed in 1887 prior to its opening to passengers. *(Plates 1 to 15).*

Section Two:
The main points of interest on a branch line were the stations, some built to NER design in use at the time of construction, but many pre-dating the formation of the NER in 1854. *(Plates 16 to 67).*

Section Three:
Trains and stations in LNER days; 1923 to 1947. *(Plates 68 to 122).*

Section Four:
Trains and stations in the BR period from 1948. *(Plates 123 to 152).*

Section Five:
A look at various features found on branch lines:
(a) Goods and mineral branches *(Plates 153 to 158).*
(b) Tyneside electrified branches *(Plates 159 to 163).*
(c) Engine sheds *(Plates 164 to 171).*
(d) Notable bridges *(Plates 172 to 178).*
(e) Signal boxes *(Plates 179 to 201).*
(f) The end *(Plates 202 to 203).*

Throughout the book, preference has been given to the passenger carrying side of the branch lines and dates quoted are normally those for passenger traffic.

Introduction

In 1905, the North Eastern Railway had ninety three branches, excluding Joint lines, carrying passenger traffic, ranging in length from the 2 miles 37 chains of the West Hartlepool to Hartlepool branch, to the 61 miles 3 chains of the Leeds Northern branch from Leeds to Stockton. These distances are, however, the distance between the stations between which the services operated and not the actual length of the branch itself. For instance, the West Hartlepool to Hartlepool service followed the West Hartlepool to Sunderland route as far as Cemetery West Junction, (1 mile 14 chains) and from that point to the terminus at Hartlepool was only 1 mile 23 chains.

The North Eastern Railway also had ninety one branches carrying only goods and/or mineral traffic, the longest being the Pontop & South Shields line from Stanhope Quarries to South Shields, a distance of 35 miles 67 chains. This branch started life in 1833 as the Stanhope & Tyne Railroad and much of it utilized steam-hauled and self-acting inclines.

On the ninety three passenger branches, the North Eastern Railway had 557 public stations with, in addition, some private stations such as Broomielaw and Hall Dene for use by nearby landowners. Some stations had separate platforms for normal and excursion traffic (Redcar, Bridlington etc.), and Newington Excursion Station only opened each October for the Hull Fair traffic. Many of the mineral and goods lines had carried a passenger service in their early days, (circa 1840 to 1860) and retained traces of platforms until quite recent times, whilst at other locations the passenger station was converted to a goods station after the passenger service had been withdrawn. A good example of this was Durham Gilesgate, which was situated at the end of the 2¼ mile branch from Belmont Junction, and which was closed to passenger traffic in 1857. However, it was used as a goods station until 1966

Although not owned by the North Eastern Railway, there were certain standard gauge privately-owned lines which made a connection with the NER and on which NER vehicles could be seen, such as the Easingwold Railway, the North Sunderland Railway and, later, the Derwent Valley Light Railway. Such lines often hired North Eastern Railway engines when a temporary replacement was required.

Many branches can be dated by the style of architecture of their stations. The work of G. T. Andrews is clearly visible on York & North Midland stations in the North and East Ridings of Yorkshire but Andrews, who was a close associate of George Hudson, the so-called 'Railway King', received no further commissions for stations after the downfall of Hudson in 1849, and thus all stations to Andrews' design were on branches opened between 1839 and 1849. Another design which crops up on various branches has stepped gables on the station buildings. Examples are Lanchester Valley (1862), Pateley Bridge branch (1862) and the Castleton to Grosmont and Grosmont to Goathland line (1865). In the 1880s, a two storey house for the stationmaster was matched with a single storey office block at each end, the latter with the gables facing on to the platform and on to the station approach. This design can be found on the Seamer to Pickering line (1882) and the Whitby West Cliff to Loftus line (1883).

From the early 1880s, far greater use was made of wood for waiting-rooms etc., which were usually built on to the brick building, and this feature could be seen throughout the North Eastern Railway system on new and rebuilt stations such an Ponteland, Ferriby and Horden. In the second half of the 1880s, a different type of gable was used, this having a flat top. It appeared at Byers Green and Coundon in May 1885 and on most stations on the Alnwick to Coldstream branch in 1887 in buildings of both single and double storey. A single storey version also appeared at Witton-le-Wear when that station was replaced in 1888.

Island platforms were never common on the North Eastern Railway but they were used, on occasions, where widening to four tracks had taken place, with two lines for the passenger trains and two for freight, for example, at Felling, South Bank and Grangetown. It was unusual to find a country station with an island platform, but one notable exception was at Whittingham, on the Alnwick to Coldstream line. Station buildings built on road bridges over the line found favour at times, as at Dinsdale (1887), which was in brick whereas Wellfield (1882) was in wood. Others were at Millfield (1890), and Cross Gates (circa 1902).

The electrification of the Tyneside branches, in the early years of the century, brought about little change. Tynemouth had been replaced, in 1882, by a fine station which easily accepted the increased service of electric trains but, because of the increased passenger traffic generated by these trains, new stations had to be provided at Whitley Bay and Monkseaton to accommodate the Newcastle businessmen who lived on the coast and who travelled daily to their place of work.

The lines to the west of the North Eastern Railway's York-Darlington-Newcastle-Berwick main line were mostly country branches, some reaching as far as the foothills of the Pennine Chain, and some piercing the barrier to reach Garsdale, Tebay and Penrith. The Newcastle & Carlisle Railway found an easier course for its line across the country using, as far as possible, the river valleys.

East of the main line the southern branches made for the east coast resorts of Bridlington, Scarborough and Whitby although, in the extreme south, the port of Hull was the objective. Further north, Middlesbrough and the River Tees were an attraction to the early railways, particularly to the Stockton & Darlington Railway and the Clarence Railway.

Many of the lines in County Durham were also making for the ports and harbours where coal could be shipped and yet, although dozens of coal trains ran daily, they were not photographed until the photography 'explosion' in the 1960s. Similarly some branches were not visited by photographers at all. Why did no one think of photographing mineral trains climbing Kelloe Bank, between Ferryhill and Hartlepool, assisted by one of the Class J73 0-6-0T engines which were stationed at Ferryhill Shed for these banking duties? The numerous North Eastern Railway inclines also escaped the early photographers, especially those transporting coal, although the remote Rosedale Incline in North Yorkshire did attract a few devoted photographers who recorded the contemporary scene.

Ravenstonedale Station, between Kirkby Stephen and Tebay, at about the turn of the century. The station was closed to passenger traffic on 1st December 1952 but the line continued to be used until January 1962.

K. L. Taylor Collection

Aysgarth Falls in Wensleydale portrayed in a poster issued by the LNER in the 1930s to publicize this beauty spot which was adjacent to the Northallerton to Hawes branch.

British Rail

AYSGARTH FALLS, YORKS.
IT'S QUICKER BY RAIL
FULL INFORMATION FROM ANY LNER OFFICE OR AGENCY

Fortunately the commercial publishers, cashing in on the postcard craze in the pre-1914 period, did turn their cameras towards the stations in both city and country and their efforts provide what is perhaps the best record of the stations on the branch lines.

My dictionary states that a railway branch line is 'a secondary route to a place or places not served by the main line' and as the North Eastern Railway's main line extended from Shaftholme Junction, north of Doncaster, to the north end of the Royal Border Bridge at Berwick (via York, Darlington and Newcastle), then all other lines were branches! However, as a point of accuracy, it must be pointed out that this was not the North Eastern Railway's main line when the company was formed in 1854. At that time it ran from Altofts Junction, north of Normanton, via York and Darlington, to Ferryhill, then to the east of the present main line, through Leamside and Washington to Pelaw and Gateshead, the original terminus. Thus it was not until the early years of this century, when the Company's working timetable was modernized, that the Normanton to York tables dropped the heading 'Main Line', and the Ferryhill-Leamside-Gateshead section ceased to be included in the 'Main Line-York and Newcastle' tables.

By 1905, the NER two volume Index of NER Acts, 1854-1904, which lists all 'Passenger Stations and their Respective Branches', 'Passenger Branches on which there is No Station', and 'Goods and Mineral Lines', treats both the Normanton to York line and Leamside line as branches, and these same two volumes have been used as guidance throughout this book.

Closure of North Eastern branch lines is nothing new as it has been going on since the company was formed in 1854. The earliest I can trace is the withdrawal of part of the Hull local service in September 1854, only a few weeks after the NER came into being! This service had been introduced by the York & North Midland Railway on 1st June 1853, but it was not a success and it was gradually withdrawn until the final section was closed in November 1854, when the takings for the remaining section for the final week were 4s 8d!

Closures were not always due entirely to poor receipts. They could also be due to changed operating conditions, or to the provision of an alternative route. The latter is illustrated by the closure of Durham Gilesgate on 1st April 1857 when a new Durham station was opened on the branch from Leamside to Bishop Auckland. Even so, Durham Station was not on the main line and it was not until the 1870s, with the opening of the Team Valley line and the extension to Ferryhill, that Durham changed in status from a branch line station to a main line station.

Even though a branch line was closed a century or more ago, many traces may still remain, particularly where engineering works such as embankments, tunnels and bridges were necessary. Except for iron bridges, where the metal had a scrap value and was worth recovering, it was not economical to fill in cuttings or tunnels which had been so laboriously excavated using only men and horses. A good example is Harrogate Brunswick Station where the tunnel leading to the station still stands although disused for 120 years. This is repeated throughout the north-east.

I must stress that the dates quoted normally refer only to passenger services. Some branch lines lasted for a century or more after the passenger traffic had been withdrawn and quoting both passenger and goods dates would have proved boring to many readers. There are various reference works available which give such dates in great detail, notably *Clinker's Register of Closed Passenger Stations and Goods Depots in England, Scotland and Wales,* for anyone who wishes to concentrate on closure dates for various classes of traffic.

A train carrying holiday-makers home from Blackpool to the north-east leaves Barnard Castle and crosses the road from Barnard Castle to Stanhope. The Blackpool trains, in both directions, were introduced in 1932 and ran during the summer months, except in World War II, until the line closed in 1962.

J. W. Armstrong

Another Blackpool train, heading east, this time with two Class J21 0-6-0 engines, leaving Tebay and passing Tebay Yard No. 3 signal box. Weight restrictions over the viaducts on the branch prevented the use of larger and more modern engines, although these restrictions were considerably eased in 1954 allowing the use of BR Class 4MT 2-6-0 locomotives. The line, which started life under the wing of the Stockton & Darlington Railway as the South Durham & Lancashire Union Railway, was opened in 1861.

J. W. Armstrong

Stations on the Alnwick to Coldstream Branch

The line from Alnwick to Coldstream served a large area of Northumberland, east of the Cheviot Hills, and for much of the way the branch ran parallel to the East Coast Main Line, but some ten miles to the west. The floating of a scheme for a Central Northumberland Railway serving much of the area, but with leanings towards the North British Railway rather than the North Eastern Railway, prompted the latter company to promote a line of their own and the two competing Bills were before Parliament in 1881/2. The North Eastern Railway was the victor and, on 19th May 1882, the Alnwick and Cornhill Act authorized a line 35 miles 2 chains 5 yds. long. At the northern end, to gain access to Berwick, the new line was to join the Tweedmouth-Sprouston-Kelso (NBR) branch at Cornhill-on-Tweed, on the English side of the River Tweed but, from 1st October 1873, the station at Cornhill had been renamed Coldstream, presumably because the latter name was better known, even though the town of Coldstream was 1½ miles away on the other side of the Tweed, and thus in Scotland.

After eighteen months of preparatory work, the contract for the construction of the line was awarded to Messrs Meakin & Dean of London, at a price of £272,266 15d 3d. The line was substantially built, with one tunnel, 351 yds. long, and with ten intermediate stations. A new station was also built at Alnwick. The station buildings were probably the best ever built by the North Eastern Railway in its sixty eight years existence, consisting of five different designs, with the size of the station depending on the size of the community it served. In two of the designs a left-hand or right-hand version could be built and one station, Whittingham, had the passenger accommodation on an island platform, with a separate house. The stations divided into a nominal classification in order of size, were:

A: Single storey, separate house
B: Island platform, separate house
C: Two storey including house
D: Two storey including house
E: Two storey including house

The line was opened throughout on 5th September 1887 but the passenger traffic was small, because of the limited number of people living in the area, and the last passenger trains ran on 22nd September 1930. However, freight and parcels traffic continued over the length of the line until it was cut by floods in October 1949. This led to abandonment of the section between Ilderton and Wooler and the branch was then worked in two parts; Alnwick to Ilderton (until March 1953) and Coldstream to Wooler (until March 1965). On the southern section, a large girder bridge over the River Breamish just north of Hedgeley Station, was recovered in 1954, for use elsewhere, and the track was then lifted. The station buildings still stand and the houses are occupied, some of them making very attractive residences standing in their own grounds. Although remote, the site of the line is easily accessible by road from Newcastle or Berwick and it runs through very attractive unspoilt countryside, making it well worth a visit.

Miles	Chains			
00	00	(Alnwick)		
7	00	Edlingham	A	Right-hand
9	70	Whittingham	B	Island
11	47	Glanton	C	Right-hand
13	44	Hedgeley	C	Left-hand
15	57	Wooperton	C	Left-hand
18	49	Ilderton	C	Right-hand
22	13	Wooler	E	
24	63	Akeld	D	
27	59	Kirknewton	A	Left-hand
32	8	Mindrum	C	Left-hand
35	55	(Coldstream)		

Through the courtesy of Mr K. L. Taylor, I am able to illustrate all the stations on the branch just after they had been completed in 1887. These unique views show how solidly they were built of stone, and the excellent workmanship. They were, however, too large for this country line which handled passengers for only forty four years.

1 The line climbed over the hills to the west of Alnwick. Edlingham had a population of 74 in 1901 and the station also served Lemmington, 1½ miles away with a population of 57. Here at Edlingham one of the smallest types of stations was provided. It was renamed Edlingham Halt from September 1926.

2 Whittingham Station served the village of the same name 1½ miles away, which had a population of 439, although the total population of the area served by the station was 885. The canopy surrounding the station buildings included some fine cast-iron work, which still remains, although all the glass has disappeared.

3 Glanton Station was a two storey building with an additional house at 90 degrees to the track. This station, along with most of the others on the branch, had extensive wood and glass lean-to erections on the platform side, to accommodate waiting-rooms etc.

4 The entrance to Glanton Station, with finishing touches being given to the garden in front of the house.

5 Hedgeley Station was similar to Glanton but opposite-handed. The photograph shows, on the extreme left, the covered lime cell at the end of the coal cells.

6 Wooperton was similar to Hedgeley, and served a number of villages and hamlets with a total population of 531. The village of Wooperton itself, situated half a mile from the station, in 1901, boasted only 57 inhabitants.

7 The exterior of Wooperton Station showing, a covered lime cell on the extreme right.

8 Ilderton Station was similar to Glanton and it is now an imposing private residence which faces across a wide lawn on to the A697 road between Morpeth and Coldstream, a road which parallels the course of the railway between Whittingham and Akeld.

9 Wooler Station, 22 miles from Alnwick, was the largest and most important station on the line, with two platforms connected by a footbridge. It served the 1,336 inhabitants of Wooler, an important market town notable for its sheep sales.

10 The entrance to the booking office at Wooler was protected from the weather by a glazed canopy which was supported on four substantial cast-iron brackets.

11 The waiting shed on the 'up' platform at Wooler.

12 Akeld station house was identical to that at Wooler, but the single storey office block was smaller, and warranted only a small canopy.

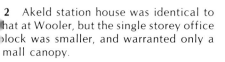

13 Kirknewton was another of the smallest stations, similar to Edlingham but built opposite handed. It served the village of the same name with only 67 inhabitants. The station was built in a cramped position between the Akeld to Kelso road and the line, with no fore court or approach road. The entrance to the station was from the grass verge.

14 Mindrum Station was similar to Hedgeley and Wooler, with the usual long glazed wooden lean-to erection. The barrow, with wicker skip, is standing on the weigh-table.

15 The fine girder bridge across the River Breamish at Hedgeley. This single span wrought iron structure, with girders 104ft. 6in. long, 10ft. 1in. high at the centre, and 2ft. 3in. wide, was dismantled after the southern section of the branch closed in 1953. The two main girders, each weighing 29½ tons, were recovered for further use by rolling them to the south side of the river and then loading them on to railway wagons.

Picture Postcards and North Eastern Branch Line Stations

The popularity of the picture postcard in the years prior to World War I led to enormous quantities being printed, covering almost every subject under the sun, and there is now a large demand for such cards. These cards command high prices as collections are added to, following a favourite 'theme'. Fortunately for railway enthusiasts and historians, the country railway station was a popular subject for the photographers taking the views for the postcard publishers, and numerous examples of these cards still exist. They continue to turn up as old postcard albums appear in salerooms throughout the country, and what at one time would be thrown away as junk, is now eagerly sought for.

Some of the cards were produced by large concerns such as Frith and Valentine, but many were sold bearing the imprint of a local stationer or photographer, who found there was a demand and was prepared to fill it. The most popular cards appear to have been the glossy cards, printed in black and white or sepia, but there were also coloured cards, where the original had been prepared by hand colouring a black and white view, and it is possible to come across identical views in black and white and in colour.

As the North Eastern Railway did not normally photograph its stations, these commercial postcards are the best contemporary record of the various stations in their heyday, usually with some members of the staff standing self-consciously in front of the station buildings. Trains do not often appear in the views, possibly because they would obscure much of the station, but often, the stationmaster's wife and children have been brought on to the platform for the occasion.

Some stations, serving holiday centres or beauty spots, warranted so many cards that reprints and new views were required, and often more than one publisher had views available. Therefore, different views exist, as many as six of some stations, with probably more to come to light.

After World War I, in the 1920s, there were fewer commercial cards and there were few railway enthusiasts photographing stations and branches. Preference was placed on train photographs so station views from that period are not too plentiful. However, more and more views of branch line trains were being taken and these increased in the 1930s. Needless to say, from the 1950s, every branch line has been photographed time and time again.

I have been collecting commercial card views of North Eastern Railway stations for many years, long before they reached their present high prices, and a number are included in the following pages.

Through the courtesy of Lens of Sutton I have also been able to reproduce a number of views from his collection.

16 Shildon (*Bishop Auckland & Weardale Branch*): Although Shildon will always be associated with the Stockton & Darlington Railway, the station illustrated was not strictly on the Stockton & Darlington Railway but on an associated line which started life as the Bishop Auckland & Weardale Railway. This was built to reach further north, towards Crook and the mineral-rich Wear Valley. The first section from Shildon to South Church was opened in 1842, passing through Shildon Tunnel (1,220 yds.). In this view, looking north, the original 1825 line to the foot of Brusselton Incline can be seen to the left of the station buildings. The train is headed by 2-4-0 No. 1240 which started life as a 4-4-0 locomotive to the design of William Bouch, the Locomotive Engineer of the Stockton & Darlington Railway.

The Station, Shildon

Wear Valley Junction

17 Wear Valley Junction *(Bishop Auckland & Weardale Branch):* The northern section of the BA&W line, from South Church to Crook, was opened in November 1843, but, although the Act included powers to build a line along the Wear Valley to Witton-le-Wear, it was not built at that time. Later, another Stockton & Darlington sponsored company was formed (the Wear Valley Railway), and in August 1847 opened its line from Wear Valley Junction to Frosterley. Wear Valley Junction was a new station on the Bishop Auckland & Weardale line, but as it was built by the Wear Valley Company, it was similar in design to the stations on the branch. Wear Valley Junction Station had an unusual layout in that the 'down' platform was south of the junction but the 'up' platform was to the north. The passenger service on the branch was, until 1935, provided by coaches from Darlington, detached from Darlington to Blackhill trains and worked from Wear Valley Junction to Wearhead by one of the branch engines. The station served a sparsely-populated area, the majority of the passengers probably coming from the nearby railway cottages which housed the staff employed at the small engine shed.

18 (below) Kenton *(Ponteland Branch):* Branching off the old Blyth & Tyne route at South Gosforth, the line to Ponteland was opened in 1905, with the hope that the area would become residential and generate enough passenger traffic to warrant electrification.

However, at the time this did not materialize (although part of the line has now been electrified by the Tyneside Metro system), and it was served by a push and pull autocar unit shuttling backwards and forwards between South Gosforth and Ponteland. Kenton, an intermediate station, was renamed Kenton Bank in 1923 and the branch passsenger traffic was withdrawn in June 1929.

KENTON STATION.

19 Dunston-on-Tyne *(Dunston Branch):* This station was opened on 1st January 1909 to serve an area west of Gateshead, and it was the terminus of an autocar service from Newcastle Central, taking eight minutes for the 2½ miles. The service was suspended for some months in World War I due to shortage of staff, and it again ceased to run in May 1926 because of the General Strike, but was never restored.

THE RAILWAY STATION, DUNSTON-ON-TYNE (230)

20 Billingham *(Stockton & Hartlepool Branch):* The Clarence Railway was built to provide a more direct route for coal traffic from the Shildon area to the River Tees, in competition with the Stockton & Darlington Railway, which made a big sweep to the south to serve Darlington and Yarm. The line was opened in 1833 but the station illustrated was built in 1866. It was renamed Billingham Junction in 1878, reverted to Billingham in 1893, and changed to Billingham-on-Tees in 1926. The photograph was taken around the turn of the century, before the signal box was replaced by a larger and much taller structure.

21 Greatham *(Stockton & Hartlepool Branch):* Immediately east of Billingham the Stockton & Hartlepool Railway branched off to the north, with intermediate stations at Greatham and Seaton Carew on the way to West Hartlepool. This view shows Greatham, on what later became an important route used by Newcastle to Liverpool trains, and the hourly Newcastle to Middlesbrough service. Seen hauling the train is a Class 398 0-6-0 locomotive. The style of the buildings on the 'down' platform suggest they were built in the 1880s, although the station opened in 1841.

22 Middleton-in-Teesdale *(Tees Valley Bran* The Tees Valley Railway, with its terminu Middleton-in-Teesdale, was the remnant c scheme for a line from Barnard Castle to Als Opened in 1868 by an independent comp the branch was about 7¾ miles long, with th intermediate stations. It was taken over by North Eastern Railway in 1882. In the 19 most trains from Middleton-in-Teesdale through to Newcastle, via Bishop Auckl Durham and Sunderland, but World Wa brought a change, resulting in a Darlingto Middleton-in-Teesdale service and remained until the line closed in Noven 1964. Although the stationmaster's hous original, the other buildings on the platf date from 1888/9. The engine shed in the foreground was closed in 1957 and demolis four years later.

23 Cotherstone *(Tees Valley Branch):* The stations on the single line branch to Middleton-in-Teesdale were small even by NER standards and this is Cotherstone. It was converted to an unstaffed halt in 1954 and was closed ten years later. The wives and families of the staff appear to have been recruited for this photographic occasion.

24 Stokesley *(North Yorkshire & Clevelar Branch):* The North Yorkshire & Clevelar Railway was built in sections, eastwards fro Picton to Castleton, reached in 1861, wi the final section on to Grosmont being cor pleted in 1865 by the North Eastern Railwa allowing a Stockton to Whitby service to k introduced. Stokesley Station, a mile sou of the market town of the same name, w the most important station on the line, bu the section between Picton and Battersb which included Stokesley, closed in Jur 1954, with the last train from Whitby Stockton worked by Class B1 4-6-0 No. 610 *Chiru.*

25 Ingleby *(North Yorkshire & Cleveland Branch):* Between Stokesley and Battersby was Ingleby where, in July 1873, new station buildings were provided at a cost of £809 6s 8d. The stationmaster and his family, and the dog, have again posed for the photographer, with the permanent way men at the other end of the platform standing well clear of the 'down' goods, headed by a Class C 0-6-0 locomotive.

26 Danby *(North Yorkshire & Cleveland Branch):* On the NER-built section of the branch east of Castleton, completed in 1865, the stone station buildings of Danby Station have the stepped gables of the period, a style also used at Goathland and on the Pateley Bridge and Lanchester Valley branches. A covered lime cell stands at the end of the coal cell line, and the water tank is made up of standard NER plates mounted on what appears to be an earlier stone base. The brick signal box probably dates from the 1870s.

27 Lealholm *(North Yorkshire & Cleveland Branch):* Lealholm was a similar station, again with the addition of a brick-built signal box, but with no water tank. In some NER records the name appears as Lealholme, but I have also seen it referred to as Lealholme Bridge.

Witton Gilbert Station.

28 Witton Gilbert *(Lanchester Valley Branch):* Another stepped gable house, but this time at Witton Gilbert on the branch between Durham and Consett, which was opened to passenger traffic in 1862 and closed in 1939.

SHOTLEY BRIDGE

29 Shotley Bridge *(Consett Branch):* For many years a service operated between Newcastle and Durham, via Scotswood, Blackhill and Consett, and Shotley Bridge was on the Scotswood to Consett section. It was closed to passengers in 1953.

The Station, Willington.

30 Willington *(Durham & Bishop Auckland Branch):* In 1857 the North Eastern Railway opened a line from Leamside, then on the York to Newcastle main line, to Bishop Auckland, where it connected with the Stockton & Darlington Railway at a Joint station. Willington was one of the stations on the branch and, at the time this picture was taken, it served a busy colliery district.

31 Newbiggin *(Newbiggin Branch):* North of the River Tyne the Blyth & Tyne Railway continued to operate as an independent concern until taken over by the North Eastern Railway in 1874. It had a network of lines primarily for carrying coal to the coast and to the north bank of the River Tyne, but it also carried passengers from Newcastle to the coastal area between Tynemouth and Newbiggin. The company had intended extending northwards to Amble, but this line was built only as far as Ashington to enable the Newbiggin branch to be completed (in 1872). Passenger services ceased in 1964.

RAILWAY STATION, NEWBIGGIN.

32 Bedlington *(Newbiggin Branch):* The Blyth & Tyne lines to Morpeth and Newbiggin diverged at Bedlington. For many years the service to Morpeth was considered of major importance, with connections provided at Bedlington for Newbiggin. However, a change to a Manors North to Newbiggin service reversed the position and passengers then needed to change for Morpeth. The latter service commenced at Blyth, with a reversal at Newsham and, in the 1930s, it was worked by the Sentinel articulated railcar *Phenomena.* The station nameboard reads 'Passengers change for North Seaton, Ashington and Newbiggin' and refers, of course, to the earlier pattern of services.

BEDLINGTON STATION.   950.

33 Shield Row *(Annfield Plain Branch):* In 1894, the North Eastern Railway provided a new route from South Pelaw to Annfield Plain, giving an alternative to the inclines built by the Stanhope & Tyne Railroad in the 1830s on its line from Stanhope Quarries to South Shields. The new route, which was extended to Consett in 1896, could be worked by locomotives, and led to the introduction, eventually, of a Newcastle-Birtley-Consett-Blackhill service, which connected with the Newcastle-Scotswood-Blackhill-Durham service. Shield Row was renamed West Stanley in 1934 and was closed in 1955.

Station, Shield Row.

STANHOPE · STATION

34 Stanhope (*Wear Valley Branch*): The lin
along the Wear Valley was extended fro
Frosterley to Stanhope in 1862 and, aft
many demands by people living at the hea
of the valley, was further extended
Wearhead in 1895. It was impossible to co
tinue the line to Wearhead from the origin
Stanhope Station so a new station had to b
built at the start of the new line. This is th
1895 station, which closed to passengers
1953. For many years the branch was worke
by engines stationed at Stanhope and We
Valley Junction sheds, but the former close
in 1930 and the latter in 1935.

35 Horden (*Durham Coast Branch*):
Until 1905 there was no route along the
coast from Hartlepool to Sunderland.
Until then, to leave the coastal strip,
trains had to climb Hesleden Bank
in one direction and Seaton Bank in
the other. By utilizing the former
Londonderry Railway, and by building
a new line between Seaham and Hart,
it was possible to complete a route
along the coast which is still in use,
although Horden Station closed in
1964. In this view, the all-wood construction is of particular interest, a
contrast to the solid stone-built stations on the Alnwick to Coldstream
branch of only twenty years earlier.

RAILWAY STATION. WYLAM.

36 Wylam (*Newcastle & Carlisle Bra*
Wylam Station retained some of its ori
buildings on the Carlisle-bound platform,
here. The Newcastle platform was on
opposite side of the level crossing, be
the over-track type of signal box, which
favoured by the North Eastern Railwa
numerous locations in County Durham
Northumberland.

37 Leamside *(Newcastle, Leamside & Ferryhill Branch):* The original East Coast Main Line, which was opened in 1844, ran via Ferryhill and Washington to Gateshead, and in 1857 a branch was opened to Durham and Bishop Auckland. There was no station at the actual junction but Leamside, situated 400 yds. to the north, became the interchange station. It was an island station with a short bay inset at each end. With the opening of the Team Valley line in 1868, and the extension to Ferryhill in 1872, the 'old main line' gradually declined and, in 1953, Leamside was closed. The buildings were then demolished and the track was straightened.

38 Fencehouses *(Newcastle, Leamside & Ferryhill Branch):* Also on the 'old main line' was Fencehouses Station, with the buildings on the 'down' side probably dating from 1844, when the line was opened, as they show traces of the hand of the architect G. T. Andrews of York. Hereabouts, the NER tracks were paralleled by tracks owned by the Lambton, Hetton & Joicey Colliery Group, and the level crossing gates over both pairs of tracks were operated from the NER signal box. This continued under British Rail/National Coal Board ownership.

39 Washington *(Newcastle, Leamside & Ferryhill Branch):* At Washington, the Durham Junction Railway joined the Pontop & South Shields route and, in early days, the latter was utilized to reach Brockley Whins and the Brandling Junction line as the East Coast Main Line was built up piecemeal by George Hudson. In 1850, a cut-off was opened from Washington to Pelaw to improve the 'old main line' but the opening of the Team Valley line eventually reduced it to the status of a branch line. Worthy of note in this view is the redundant signal box and its replacement.

40 Haltwhistle (*Newcastle & Carlisle Branch*): Haltwhistle became the junction for the line to Alston when the first part of the branch was opened in 1851. In this view, the branch train can be seen standing at the outside face of the wide island platform, which accommodated trains for Carlisle on its opposite face. The 'up' platform is beyond the goods shed. The nearest bridge over the River South Tyne carried the minor road to Lambley, where the Brampton to Alston road was joined, and the far bridge carried the Alston branch line. Long overdue road improvements allowed the Alston branch to be closed in 1976.

41 Murton (*Stockton & Sunderland Branch*): The two Durham & Sunderland lines diverged at Murton, one to Shincliffe (later to Durham Elvet), and the other to Haswell, to meet the Hartlepool Dock & Railway's line. At first, there was no physical connection between the two lines at Haswell, as they were at different levels, but later, a primitive connection was installed, and in 1877, with further improvements at Haswell, the two lines were converted into a through route between Newcastle, Sunderland and Hartlepool. The station at Murton was in the 'V' of the junction, and this view shows a train from Sunderland leaving the southbound platform.

42 Castle Eden (*Stockton & Sunderland Branch*): Castle Eden was situated on the Hartlepool Dock & Railway's section of the same route. In the distance the old A19 road crosses the line on the overbridge, which hides the northbound platform. Arriving at the 'up' platform is a North Eastern Railway autocar, easily distinguishable by the portholes in the driving compartment of the coach, which is being propelled by a BTP engine.

43 Carlton *(Ferryhill & Stockton Branch):* Between Carlton West Junction and Stillington North Junction, the old Clarence Railway of 1835 became part of the Shildon to Newport line on which electric traction was introduced in 1915. Widening to four tracks in the 1880s, to accommodate the increased mineral traffic, led to Carlton being rebuilt as an island platform station between the 'up' and 'down' passenger lines. The alteration was authorized in January 1884 at a cost of £525 18s 9d. Under the plethora of renamings in the early days of the LNER, Carlton became Redmarshall.

44 Benton *(Blyth & Tyne Branch):* The first NER electrification took place in the Newcastle area in 1904, utilizing the old Blyth & Tyne main line out of New Bridge Street Station at Newcastle, to serve the residential area of Jesmond, Gosforth and Benton, en route to the coast at Monkwearmouth, Whitley Bay and Tynemouth, and then back to Newcastle Central. However, a Central to Central circular working was not introduced until 1917, eight years after New Bridge Street Station had been replaced by Manors North and through running had become possible. In 1900 a curve from the Blyth & Tyne line at Benton, to the East Coast Main Line south of Forest Hall, was authorized, but it was not built. However, as this 1904 view shows, the signals for the curve were installed and are here 'crossed' out of use. The curve was eventually opened in 1940 as a wartime measure.

45 Backworth *(Blyth & Tyne Branch):* A train from New Bridge Street Station prepares to depart from Backworth Station. The line to Morpeth and Newbiggin diverges immediately beyond the overbridge, on which a new booking office has been built. The electric trains were originally in a red and cream livery, which lasted until 1920. The rear driving cab has had the glass removed and replaced by a panel having a circular spectacle.

46 Lartington *(South Durham & Lancashire Union Branch):* Lartington was one of the substantial stations on the line from Barnard Castle to Tebay, which was opened in 1861. This line climbed over the Pennines at Stainmore and dropped down into Westmorland, through Barras, famous for the amount of snow it received.

47 Kirkby Thore *(Eden Valley Branch):* From the South Durham line at Kirkby Stephen a line went off to Penrith, although it originally joined the London & North Western Railway at Clifton, south of Penrith. This was the Eden Valley Branch, serving the market town of Appleby, where connection was made with the Midland Railway's Settle and Carlisle route. Kirkby Thore was closed in 1953 and has since completely disappeared under road improvements as the busy A66 road ran past the front of the station.

N.E. R^{ly} STATION N° 21
KIRKBYTHORE WESTMORLAND

WARCOP 10

48 Warcop *(Eden Valley Branch):* Also on the Eden Valley branch was Warcop seen here before a new signal box was erected at the far end of the platform.

49 Askrigg *(Hawes Branch):*   A view of Askrigg Station situated in Wensleydale, a very picturesque part of Yorkshire.

ASKRIGG. NER.

AYSGARTH. NER.

50 Aysgarth *(Hawes Branch):* This station, also in Wensleydale, was near the famous River Ure falls and attracted numerous visitors. However, this party looks as if it is going off for the day. Posters in the background advertise circular tours, 1,000 mile tickets, the resort of Scarborough and the town of Hexham.

51 Pateley Bridge *(Nidd Valley Branch):* Still in the Yorkshire Dales, but this time in Nidderdale, was Pateley Bridge Station, with the branch train seen in the platform. In 1907 an end-on connection with the NER branch was made by the Nidd Valley Light Railway, which was built to supply reservoirs under construction at the head of the valley. The line was owned by Bradford Corporation and until 1st January 1930, it carried a passenger service between Pateley Bridge and Lofthouse. Unusual motive power included Metropolitan 4-4-0T locomotives and a former Great Western Railway steam railcar.

PATELEY BDGE. NER.

52 Hovingham Spa *(Thirsk & Malton Branch):* The li■ from Pilmoor to Malton was, for most of its existence ■ quiet country branch but in the summer months, in LN■ and BR days, it regularly saw Class B1, B16, and ■ locomotives, and occasionally Pacifics, on the Saturd■ Glasgow and Newcastle to Scarborough trains. T■ normal passenger service was withdrawn from 1■ January 1931 but the Scarborough trains continued to r■ until 1962, except during World War II.

53 Hayburn Wyke *(Scarborough & Whitby Branch):* This single line branch, owned by the Scarborough & Whitby Railway was opened in 1885 but, from the outset, was worked by the North Eastern Railway. The platform was originally on the opposite side of the track. Hayburn Wyke closed from March 1917 to May 1921 as a wartime measure, was downgraded to an unstaffed halt in March 1955, and closed completely in March 1965.

The Station, Hayburn Wyke.

54 Robin Hood's Bay *(Scarborough ■ Whitby Branch):* The most importan■ station on the Scarborough & Whitb■ line was Robin Hood's Bay. The rout■ was notable for its steep gradients an■ sharp curves. Traffic was heavy wit■ holiday-makers in the summer months■ but light in the winter months whe■ only the residents used the line.

55 Sandsend *(Saltburn & Whitby Branch):* North of Whitby the coast route was started by the Whitby, Redcar & Middlesbrough Union Railway, but financial difficulties led to the Company asking the North Eastern Railway to complete the line. This proved to be a major task, and the line was not opened until December 1883. In places the line ran close to the sea and it was notable for its metal viaducts, which were necessary to carry the line across the valleys which ran down to the sea. The name of the station (and the village) is particularly apt as there is a magnificent stretch of sandy beach all the way from Whitby to Sandsend. Sandsend Ness, disfigured by alum workings, is seen in the background.

View of Sandsend & Bay

Kettleness Station.   No. 1580.

56 Kettleness *(Saltburn & Whitby Branch):* Between Sandsend and the next station, Kettleness, the line was planned to run along the cliffs, passing through five short tunnels in less than a mile, piercing the rocky outcrops. Shortage of funds led to postponement of the work and when it was resumed by the NER, a course further inland was chosen, through Sandsend tunnel (1,652 yds.) and Kettleness tunnel (308 yds.). The small signal box carries its nameboard in an unusual position, under the eaves, and prominent is the oval telegraph fault board.

57 Staithes *(Saltburn & Whitby):* This station served an important fishing village, which sometimes caught enough fish to warrant a special train to Darlington. Staithes Viaduct, 152ft. above Roxby Beck, consisted of six 60ft. and eleven 30ft. spans, and warranted a wind gauge. If the gauge registered a high velocity, trains had to stop running over the viaduct. The similarity to the buildings at Kettleness is noticeable, although Staithes signal box was at the south end of the 'up' platform, just behind the photographer.

58 Heighington (*Stockton & Darlingt*
Branch): It was at this location t
Locomotion was put on the rails af
travelling by road from Newcastle. T
station buildings, with the low platform
front, are of early Stockton & Darlingt
Railway design but it is doubtful if they
back as far as 1825. The buildings a
because of a fall in the land, single storey
the platform, but two storey at the back, a
are currently being converted into a pub
house.

59 Kirkby Stephen (*South Durham &*
Lancashire Union Branch): A line
which was backed by the Stockton &
Darlington Railway was the South
Durham & Lancashire Union Railway
from Bishop Auckland to Tebay and
the first section, from Barnard Castle
to Tebay, was opened in 1861. The
most important intermediate station
was Kirkby Stephen, with its island
platform and a single line train shed on
each side. There was also a small
engine shed with its own water-
powered electricity generating plant,
but now all has disappeared except
the station buildings which are in use
for industrial purposes. The engine on
the right is one of the Stockton &
Darlington long-boilered 0-6-0 locomotives of which one has survived for
preservation.

60 Barras (*South Durham & Lancash*
Union Branch): This remote stati
situated on the western slopes of t
Pennines, was noted for its snow-dri
and, during bad winters, the line w
closed for weeks at a time.

61 Cross Gates *(Leeds & Selby Branch):*
The Leeds & Selby Railway opened in
1834 when Cross Gates was a village
situated some miles outside Leeds. Now
the urban sprawl has joined the two
and, although the line was widened in
1905, necessitating a new station at Cross
Gates, it has since reverted to two tracks,
but still using the platforms illustrated.

CROSS GATES, N.E.R.

62 Garforth *(Leeds & Selby Branch):*
This is an area which has developed
extensively since World War II, but
this photograph was taken during the
first ten years of this century when
Garforth was a village dominated by
colliery workings, some of which were
served by the colliery-owned Aberford
Railway. This line carried a passenger
service for many years, but closed in
1924.

63 Brough *(Hull & Selby Branch):*   The Hull &
Selby Railway completed a link in the line of
railways across the country from Liverpool to
Hull when it was opened in 1840. Traffic to Hull,
from the Leeds and Doncaster directions, shared
the same tracks from Staddlethorpe, which
resulted in that stretch of line being widened
to four tracks. Brough was the only station to
have platforms to all four tracks. At the west
end of Brough, the original station building
was allowed to remain when widening took
place, although the house had to be cut back to
allow the 'down' slow line to be laid. The old
house is on the left and is the white building
with the gable.

BROUGH STATION. H.B.153

64 Ebberston *(Pickering & Seamer Branch):* This branch was opened in 1882 and closed in 1950. In the 1930s, it was worked by a Sentinel steam railcar in an effort to reduce costs, and eventually a Class G5 0-4-4T, on a push and pull set, took over. The station was much nearer Allerston than Ebberston and, until 1903, it was known as Wilton.

65 Snainton *(Pickering & Seamer Branch):* This station served a fairly large village but closed in 1950 with the remainder of the branch. The *Yorkshire Herald* contents board in the background proclaims 'Govt. Threaten Unionist Leaders. Churchill again! Land Tax Plot'.

66 Eston *(Eston Branch):* The North Eastern Railway opened a station at Eston in 1902, although, for some time, a passenger service of sorts had been provided over Bolckow Vaughan's private lines. This was used mainly on a Saturday night to carry home Eston residents who had been spending the evening in Middlesbrough. The North Eastern Railway trains ran over the former Cleveland and Stockton & Darlington lines between Eston and Middlesbrough, but it was a short-lived service which was withdrawn in March 1929.

67 Flatts Lane Level Crossing *(Eston Branch):* A train bound for Middlesbrough comes off the new section of line built by the NER, and is about to join the former Cleveland Railway route between Guisborough and the River Tees near Cargo Fleet.

Branch Lines in the LNER Period

On 1st January 1923, the LNER took over the extensive North Eastern Railway system but obviously could not initiate changes immediately and these were introduced gradually. The earliest signs of change appear to have been on posters, handbills and notices which, by their content, were not printed until required for display, and these soon were headed by the initials or name of the new company. Printed stationery, of which there must have been large stocks, often had LONDON AND imprinted by rubber stamp before the words NORTH EASTERN RAILWAY. Soon the engines and coaches started to appear in their new colours, with many passenger engines retaining a green livery (darker than NER green), but with their large brass numberplates removed. The coaches went into the teak finish but the goods wagons appeared little changed as they carried only the letters N E, even if they had formerly belonged to the North Eastern, Great Northern, Great Central, North British, or other LNER constituents.

The North Eastern Railway's enamelled station nameboards were allowed to remain, but similar nameboards on the front of signal boxes were removed and new black and white boards were affixed at each end of the boxes. The branch train services continued to run at roughly the same times, with minor alterations to provide better connections as train services were accelerated after World War 1. The stationmasters changed their uniforms, and sported a different type of peaked cap, and the buttons on all uniforms carried the new initials. However, for some years, the changes were only minor and the branches continued to serve the public, although admittedly the public were not using the branch lines as much as they had done, and traffic was declining.

Signs of economies to come were obvious when a start was made in painting the secondary passenger engines black instead of green, and in the early 1930s, engines which were not required for use were placed in store. Staff were dismissed or reduced in grade, causing many footplatemen to leave the Locomotive Department to act as porters etc.

However, throughout the 1930s most of the branch lines continued much as before, although some services were pruned, with perhaps a long-established late train running only on Saturdays, so that the branch could close earlier. Some branches lost their Sunday services, although some branches had a Sunday service for the first time. This occurred in seaside and holiday areas where Sunday traffic was encouraged in the summer months to bring in extra revenue.

Also in the 1930s, the main line saw the introduction of streamlined locomotives and trains, but the branch lines continued to use former North Eastern Railway engines and coaches, many, by then, forty years old. Corridor coach sets, including buffet cars, appeared on some of the major branches, such as Scarborough-York-Leeds and Newcastle to Carlisle, in an attempt to woo customers with improved facilities. However, the less important branches did not get this treatment.

Regular interval services were introduced, notably in the Hull area, to make the train times easier to remember and, from 1932, many services were accelerated, although there was little that could be done with branch line trains stopping at every station. The LNER experimented with new forms of transport and traction with a view to saving money and improving efficiency, notably with steam and diesel railcars, although in the late 1930s, the Company reverted to steam-worked push and pull units, similar to those which had operated on so many NER branch lines from 1905.

The steam railcars were of two types, Sentinel and Clayton, and they were extensively used on branch lines all over the north-east, although it must be admitted that the Clayton cars were not a great success. Although the Sentinel cars were more reliable they did spend long periods out of traffic, under repair or awaiting spare parts. Sheds with a stud of railcars inevitably had spare cars to cover failures, and sheds with only one car had to provide a locomotive-hauled train when its car was not available. On some branches the service was provided entirely by railcars, but on others railcars appeared only on a particular service, or on a filling-in turn. Occasionally, they were hired by special parties, but on journeys of any distance, they had to stop at intermediate stations as the cars had no toilet facilities!

The diesel-electric cars, which were built by Armstrong Whitworth & Co., were used to give an improved service on certain branches. The Hull car, for instance, worked to Pontefract to connect with York-Sheffield-West of England trains, and the Leeds car worked express services between Leeds-York-Harrogate-Leeds. The Middlesbrough car was used to replace a normal train on the line to Scarborough, but only in the winter months when the number of passengers was within its capacity. In the summer months it was used on a circular tour from Scarborough to Whitby, via Pickering and Grosmont, returning after lunch via Ravenscar.

World War II affected the branch lines severely. In the early days of the war, when no one knew what was going to happen, many branch line services were cut to the bone, but when things settled down most services were increased, although not necessarily back to pre-war level. A few branches saw increased traffic, and some saw passenger trains for the first time. A munition factory at Thorp Arch brought many extra trains carrying workpeople, especially from the West Riding, and to serve the Royal Ordnance Factory near Aycliffe, the Simpasture Junction to Stillington North Junction section of the old Clarence Railway's Simpasture branch saw passenger trains three times a day as the shifts changed. The Masham branch was notable for the amount of munition traffic which it handled as shells were sent for storage on the grass verges of the country lanes, and then were reloaded on their way to the Second Front. Notable, also, was the Richmond branch, familiar to thousands of men and women who were based at, or passed through, Catterick Camp.

When the LNER took over, only one branch had been closed since 1900, namely the short Coxhoe (WH) branch, which last appeared in the timetable for March 1902. However, the first branch to go after the LNER had taken over was the 1¼ mile Brampton Town branch, which had never been a success since the North Eastern Railway took it over in 1913.

The Dunston branch service was a casualty in 1926, its end hastened by the General Strike, but it was the closure of the Eston branch on 11th March 1929 that started a run of closures of uneconomical lines, such as the South Gosforth-Ponteland-Darras Hall, Cawood, Amble, Allendale, Alnwick to Coldsteam, Pittington to Durham Elvet, Malton to Gilling, Masham, and Stockton to Wellfield branches, which had all gone by the end of 1931. However, it must be stressed that goods, mineral and parcels traffic continued to be carried on most of these lines, together with occasional excursion trains.

It will be noticed that most of the branches mentioned were built or opened to passenger traffic after 1880, and it will generally be found that the last branches to be built were the first to be closed to passengers.

Another wave of line closures started in 1939, such as Tow Law to Consett, the Lanchester Valley branch, with the branches to Port Clarence, Seaham Harbour, and Ferryhill to Bishop Auckland losing part of the line. After that, the system continued with little change until British Railways' inspired closures began.

Four NER services which have disappeared, originally shown in the 1902 timetable.

HARTLEPOOL AND FERRYHILL.

Light Type a.m.   Dark Type—p.m.

WEEKDAYS.

					A						A
HARTLEPOOL	dep	4 10	7 20	9 10	12 48	1 18	5 0	6 3	7 43	10 44
W. HARTLEPOOL	,,	4 25	7 35	9 27	1 0	1 29	5 10	6 14	8 5	10 58
Hart	,,		7 42	9 34	1 7	1 36	5 18	6 21	8 13	
Hesleden	,,		7 50	9 42	1 15	1 44	5 27	6 30	8 21	11 14
Castle Eden	,,		7 54	9 46	1 19	1 48	5 31	6 34	8 25	11 19
Wingate	,,		7 58	9 50	1 23	1 52	5 36	6 39	8 29	11 25
Trimdon	,,		8 3	9 55	1 28	1 58	5 41	6 44	8 34	11 30
Coxhoe Bridge	,,		8 10	10 2	1 35	2 5	5 49	6 52	8 41	
West Cornforth	,,		8 15	10 7	1 40	2 10	5 55	6 58	8 46	
FERRYHILL	arr	5 0	8 20	10 12		2 15	6 0	7 3	8 51	

WEEKDAYS.

					A					
FERRYHILL	dep	5 35	8 38	11 58		3 25	6 45	8 9	9 17
West Cornforth	,,		8 43	12 3	1 50	3 30	6 50	8 14	9 22
Coxhoe Bridge	,,		8 47	12 7	1 54	3 34	6 54	8 18	9 26
Trimdon	,,		8 57	12 17	2 4	3 44	7 4	8 28	9 36
Wingate	,,		9 2	12 22	2 9	3 49	7 9	8 33	9 41
Castle Eden	,,		9 6	12 26	2 14	3 53	7 13	8 37	9 45
Hesleden	,,		9 10	12 30	2 18	3 57	7 17	8 41	9 49
Hart	,,		9 16	12 36	2 24	4 3	7 23	8 47	
W. HARTLEPOOL	arr	6 17	9 34	12 42	2 30	4 19	7 29	8 53	10 0
HARTLEPOOL	,,	6 27	9 24	12 56	3 20	4 9	7 48	9 6	10 12

A Saturdays only.

		SUN.				SUNDAYS.	
HARTLEPOOL	dep	6 35	5 5	FERRYHILL	dep	5 35	8 55	9 7
W. HARTLEPOOL	,,	6 50	4 45	West Cornforth	,,		9 0	9 13
Hart	,,	6 57	5 12	Coxhoe Bridge	,,		9 4	9 18
Hesleden	,,	7 5	5 20	Trimdon	,,		9 14	9 29
Castle Eden	,,	7 9	5 24	Wingate	,,		9 19	9 35
Wingate	,,	7 13	5 28	Castle Eden	,,		9 23	9 39
Trimdon	,,	7 18	5 33	Hesleden	,,		9 27	9 43
Coxhoe Bridge	,,	7 25	5 40	Hart	,,		9 33	9 49
West Cornforth	,,	7 30	5 45	W. HARTLEP'L	arr	6 17	9 49	10 5
FERRYHILL	arr	7 35	5 50	HARTLEPOOL	,,	6 27	9 39	9 55

MIDDLETON-IN-TEESDALE AND BARNARD CASTLE.

WEEKDAYS.

								A
MIDDLETON-IN-TEESDALE	dep	6 45	8 15	12 2	2 22	5 40	8 15
Mickleton	,,	6 49	8 19	12 6	2 26	5 44	8 19
Romaldkirk	,,	6 54	8 24	12 11	2 31	5 49	8 24
Cotherstone	,,	7 0	8 30	12 17	2 37	5 55	8 30
BARNARD CASTLE	arr	7 7	8 37	12 24	2 44	6 2	8 37

WEEKDAYS.

						A	B	C
BARNARD CASTLE	dep	7 42	11 13	1 33	4 43	6 25	9 16	9 40
Cotherstone	,,	7 49	11 20	1 40	4 50	6 32	9 23	9 47
Romaldkirk	,,	7 55	11 26	1 46	4 56	6 38	9 29	9 53
Mickleton	,,	8 0	11 31	1 51	5 1	6 43	9 34	9 58
MIDDLETON-IN-TEESDALE	arr	8 5	11 36	1 56	5 6	6 48	9 39	10 3

A Will not run after 13th September. **B** Tuesdays and Thursdays only ; commencing 15th September will run daily. **C** Tuesdays and Thursdays excepted ; will not run after 13th September.

BISHOP AUCKLAND AND FERRYHILL.

Light Type a.m.   Dark Type—p.m.

WEEKDAYS

BISHOP AUCKLAND	dep	6 40	8 0	8 49	11 17	1 43
Coundon	,,	6 46	8 6	8 55	11 23	1 49
Byers Green	,,	6 51	8 10	9 0	11 28	1 54
Spennymoor	arr	6 58	8 15	9 5	11 33	1 59
	dep		8 16	9 7	10 0	11 35	2 1	3 0	4 0
FERRYHILL	arr	8 25	9 16	10 9	11 44	2 10	3 9	4 10

WEEKDAYS —continued.

					A		B	
BISHOP AUCKLAND	dep	3 57	5 55	7 18	8 35	11 0
Coundon	,,	4 3	6 1	7 24	8 41	11 6
Byers Green	,,	4 8	6 6	7 29	8 46	11 11
Spennymoor	arr	4 13	6 11	7 34	8 51	11 18
	dep	4 15	6 13	6 50	7 36	8 53	11 19
FERRYHILL	arr	4 24	6 22	6 59	7 45	9 2	11 28

WEEKDAYS

FERRYHILL	dep		8 49	9 43	10 25	12 5	2 40	3 32	4 53
Spennymoor	arr		8 59	9 53	10 35	12 15	2 50	3 42	5 3
	dep	7 12	10 37	12 17	2 52		5 5
Byers Green	,,	7 19	9 9	10 44	12 24	2 59	5 12
Coundon	,,	7 24	9 14	10 49	12 29	3 4	5 17
BISHOP AUCKLAND	arr	7 29	9 19	10 54	12 34	3 9	5 22

WEEKDAYS —continued.

		A					
FERRYHILL	dep	6 10	6 33	7 20	9 23	10 0
Spennymoor	arr	6 20	6 43	7 30	9 33	10 10
	dep	6 21		7 32	9 35	10 11
Byers Green	,,	6 28		7 39	9 42	10 18
Coundon	,,	6 33		7 44	9 47	10 23
BISHOP AUCKLAND	arr	6 38		7 49	9 52	10 28

A Saturdays only   **B** Wednesdays only.

BISHOP AUCKLAND AND BARNARD CASTLE.

WEEKDAYS

BISHOP AUCKLAND	dep	6 53	10 5	12 22	4 0	6 56	8 32
West Auckland	,,	7 0	10 12	12 29	4 7	7 3	8 39
Evenwood	,,	7 8	10 20	12 37	4 15	7 11	8 47
Cockfield	,,	7 17	10 29	12 46	4 24	7 20	8 56
BARNARD CASTLE	arr	7 32	10 44	1 3	4 39	7 35	9 11

WEEKDAYS

								A
BARNARD CASTLE	dep	7 9	8 38	12 45	2 50	4 35	6 18	7 44
Cockfield	,,	7 26	8 55	1 2	3 7	4 53	6 34	8 0
Evenwood	,,	7 32	9 1	1 8	3 13	4 59	6 40	8 6
West Auckland	,,	7 39	9 8	1 15	3 20	5 6	6 46	8 12
BISHOP AUCKLAND	arr	7 46	9 15	1 22	3 27	5 13	6 53	8 19

A Wednesdays and Saturdays only ; will not run after 30th August.

Trains shown in italics do not run daily throughout the period for which this time table is issued

68 (above left) Ripon *(Leeds Northern Branch):* The Masham branch diverged at Melmerby, three miles north of Ripon, but most trains ran between Ripon and Masham. This scene shows an 0-4-4T, No. 1911, the Masham engine, standing at the 'down' platform at Ripon and about to depart for Melmerby.

69 (below left) Waterhouses *(Dearness Valley Branch):* This branch terminus was actually at the colliery village of Esh Winning, in the Dearness (or Deerness) Valley. Although the branch closed to regular passenger traffic in October 1951, it continued to be used one day a year for the Durham Miners' Gala festivities. The colours on the enamelled station nameboard are reversed and are chocolate letters on a cream background, with a cream border.

70 Hartlepool *(Ferryhill & Hartlepool Branch):* In LNER days, the passenger service between Hartlepool and West Hartlepool was worked by Sentinel steam railcars, but, on Saturdays, Hartlepool Shed provided two engines to work local trains. As the shed had no passenger engines, use had to be made of the shed's brake-fitted Class N8 0-6-2T engines, such as No. 961, seen standing in Hartlepool Station. This station building dated from 1878 and was closed to regular passenger traffic in June 1947, although trains for schoolchildren ran until March 1964.

71 West Auckland *(Bishop Auckland & Barnard Castle Branch):* This station was unusual in having the two platform faces both facing in the same direction, with a small footbridge over the 'down' line joining the two. This view is of a train bound for Bishop Auckland arriving at the 'up' platform, with the 'down' platform on the left.

72 (above left) Driffield *(Hull & Scarborough Branch)*: After moving from the Great Eastern Railway in 1885, T. W. Worsdell's first design for the North Eastern Railway was a neat 2-4-2T locomotive, and sixty of these were built between 1886 and 1892. When this photograph was taken, No. 1581 was working from Malton Shed on the branch to Driffield, where it is seen running round its one coach train and about to take water at the water-crane in the background, before returning to Malton.

73 (below left) Whitby *(Whitby Branch)*: In 1907/8 the North Eastern Railway built ten 4-6-0T locomotives for the hilly routes around Whitby, but they were not too successful until they were rebuilt to 4-6-2T from 1914. No. 691 was, for some time, a Whitby engine and is seen here on a set of North Eastern Railway coaches.

74 (above) Ferryhill *(Ferryhill & Stockton Branch)*: Although this view was taken outside the main line station, it shows a branch line train, with No. 2146, a Saltburn Class H1 4-4-4T

75 (below) Coxhoe Bridge *(Ferryhill & Hartlepool Branch)*: The Class H1 4-4-4T locomotives were all rebuilt to Class A8 4-6-2T in the 1930s and, in their new form, they performed a lot of good work. This is No. 9862 (ex-2155) on a Ferryhill to West Hartlepool train in 1947.

78 (above right) Hull (Paragon): Dairycoates Shed often provided Class J21 0-6-0 locomotives to work local passenger trains and to act as station pilots, although Botanic Gardens Shed was the passenger engine shed for Hull. Here No. 963, one of the three Class J21 engines rebuilt with larger boilers, is about to depart with a set of empty coaches.

79 (below right) Wearhead *(Wear Valley Branch):* The single platform station at Wearhead was opened in 1895 when the branch was extended from Stanhope. There was a small engine shed for one engine, and for years, this was used by the branch engine, a Class J21, No. 5064 (ex-314).

76 Kirkby Stephen *(South Durham & Lancashire Union Branch):* The North Eastern Railway's 0-6-0 locomotives were a hardy breed, and were often used on passenger trains, such as this Newcastle to Barrow excursion in the 1930s. Because of weight limits on the viaducts on the Stainmore line, large engines were not permitted and consequently the Class J21 locomotives had to be used in pairs on these excursions. On this occasion, the engines were Nos. 1323 and 1565.

77 Kirkby Stephen: On the daily workings, one engine sufficed as the loads were light. On this particular train, the 6p.m. from Kirkby Stephen to Tebay, the summer load was three coaches and the winter load was one coach. The engine, Class J21 No. 5119 (ex-1811), was, at that time, 53 years old, and it ran for a further seven years before being scrapped.

82 (above right) Beverley *(Hull & Scarborough Branch):* Class D17/2 4-4-0, No. 1922 leaves Beverley for Hull on a train from Bridlington, with driver W. Nicholson of Bridlington at the controls. This class of North Eastern 4-4-0 was fitted with a clerestory to the cab roof.

83 (below right) Filey *(Hull & Scarborough Branch):* The most numerous North Eastern Railway 4-4-0 locomotives were the Class D20 engines, of which sixty were built between 1899-1907. No. 707 is about to leave Filey, with the train shed in the background. This was designed by the architect, G. T. Andrews, of York, and it dates from the opening of the line in 1846. The station is still open but the roof has been partially dismantled.

80 Withernsea *(Withernsea Branch):* At the Grouping, the North Eastern Railway handed over 186 4-4-0 locomotives, including five ex-Hull & Barnsley engines, and they were used on branches throughout the system. Particularly useful in the Hull area were the Class D22 engines, first introduced in 1887, of which Botanic Gardens Shed had an allocation of sixteen in 1926. This is No. 777, later transferred to Waskerley, at Withernsea, with, in the background, a wagon owned by a firm of coal merchants in Hull. Alderman Bannister, one time Mayor of Hull, was the power behind the Hull & Holderness Railway, which was opened from Hull to Withernsea in 1854.

81 Scarborough *(York & Scarborough Branch):* Leaving Scarborough on a mixed set of coaches is Class D17/1, No. 1637, shortly after its transfer from Tweedmouth Shed to Selby in 1925. Livery is LNER green, with the number on the tender, which it lost a few years later when North Eastern Railway's 4-4-0 locomotives were painted black with red lining.

84 Harrogate *(Leeds Northern Branch)*: The Leeds & Thirsk Railway developed into the Leeds Northern Railway when extended to Stockton in 1852. In LNER days, it formed part of an important route from Leeds to Newcastle, carrying Liverpool to Newcastle trains which ran via Sunderland, and Pullman trains which ran via Darlington. Some of the Liverpool trains were handled north of Leeds by Neville Hill allocated Class D49 4-4-0 locomotives, including No. 327 *Warwickshire*, seen here approaching Harrogate Station from the north.

85 Harrogate: North of Harrogate, the Pullman trains were invariably worked by Heaton or Gateshead allocated engines, such as C7 class 4-4-2 No. 2211 of Heaton, seen between Dragon Junction and Harrogate Station. Particularly noticeable is the cleanliness of the engine and the stock.

86 Bramhope Tunnel *(Leeds Northern Branch):* The major engineering work on the Leeds & Thirsk Railway was Bramhope Tunnel (3,761 yds.) which was situated between Arthington and Horsforth. Class D49 4-4-0 No. 245 *Lincolnshire* emerges into the sunshine at the south end of the tunnel on an 'up' express.

87 (right) Bramhope Tunnel: The portal at the southern end of the tunnel was plain but the northern portico was embellished with castellated towers. This memorial in Otley Churchyard represents the northern portal and it was erected in memory of the men who were killed in the construction of the tunnel, which was opened in July 1849.

88 Smardale Viaduct *(South Durham & Lancash*
Union Branch): Although the North East
Railway carried a large number of passenge
it was the goods and mineral traffic that v
the lifeblood of the Company. To work t
the Company had 752 0-6-0 locomotives at
Grouping, comprising eight NER and two Hul
Barnsley classes. This picturesque view was tak
in Smardale, with two 0-6-0 engines in charge; c
at the head of the train and the other, banking,
the rear.

90 (above right) Stockton *(Leeds Northern Branc*
This out-of-gauge special from Darlington
Middlesbrough was carrying some 625 tons
castings for the stern frame of the new Cunard li
which was being built at Clydebank, and wh
became famous as the *Queen Mary*. The casti
were carried by rail on the first part of their journ
on 28th September 1931 and were then shipped
the Clyde.

91 (below right) Darlington: For use on
branches which suffered from heavy snowfa
large snowploughs were stationed at vari
strategic locations. They were usually marshal
in pairs, back to back, with one or two 0-6-0 lo
motives in between. However, in this examp
probably specially posed for the press pho
grapher, only one Class J24 0-6-0 locomotive
between the ploughs.

89 (below) Hylton *(Penshaw Branch):* When the north-east was a major shipbuilding
centre, out-of-gauge loads were fairly common as large castings and forgings were
conveyed from the manufacturers to the shipyards. In this scene, Class J25 0-6-0 No.
1724 passes Hylton on an out-of-gauge special from Tyne Dock to Pallion in May
1926.

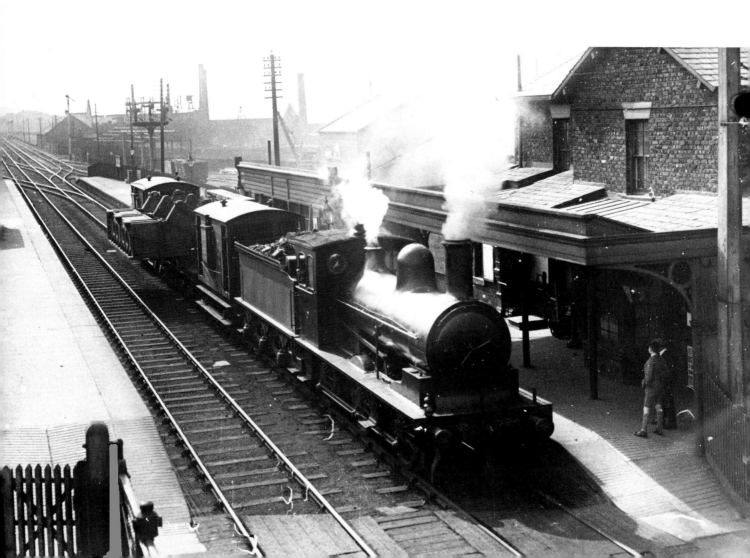

92 Beverley *(Hull & Scarborough Branch):* The most numerous North Eastern Railway 0-6-0 locomotives were the 201 of Class J21, which were used throughout the area on goods and passenger work. Many of them were fitted with Westinghouse and/or vacuum brake. This is No. 665, on a light pick-up goods, heading for Hull.

93 Norton-On-Tees *(Stockton & Hartlepool Branch):* There were also 165 0-6-0 locomotives with 5ft. 6in. diameter boilers, which became LNER Classes J26 and J27. These were particularly useful on the mineral trains in County Durham and Northumberland and were never really common in the southern parts of the system. Class J27, No. 5787 was photographed at Norton in September 1947, with its new LNER number which it received in December 1946.

94 Carlisle *(Newcastle & Carlisle Branch)*: Numerous locomotives which were designed by Edward Fletcher, who retired in 1882 from the post of Locomotive Superintendent, were taken over by the LNER, including 86 Class 398 0-6-0 engines. One of these, No. 45, is seen passing London Road Shed, Carlisle, with a brake van. The photograph was taken about 1924 and the engine was withdrawn in December 1925.

95 Cottingham South *(Hull & Scarborough Branch)*: The allocation of former Railway Operating Department's 2-8-0 locomotives to the Hull & Barnsley section displaced many of the Stirling-designed 0-6-0 engines to North Eastern sheds, such as Whitby, West Hartlepool, Shildon, Stockton and Scarborough, whilst others simply moved from the H&B to the NER shed at Hull. Here we see No. 2473 approaching Hull on a lengthy goods train.

98 (above) Botanic Gardens *(Victoria Dock Branch):* In the Hull area, numerous 'trip' workings were necessary to transfer wagons between yards and docks, and tank engines were often employed on these trains. This engine, Class N10 0-6-2T, No. 1112, was fitted with 4ft. 7¼ in. diameter wheels and Westinghouse and vacuum brakes. Normally this size of wheel was used on mineral engines without automatic brakes.

99 (below) Cottingham South *(Hull & Scarborough Branch):* Also used on Hull duties were the former Hull & Barnsley tank engines, such as Class N11, No. 2480, which was ordered originally by the Lancashire, Derbyshire & East Coast Railway, but not taken up, and was sold by the makers, Kitson & Co., to the Hull & Barnsley Railway in 1901.

96 (above left) Norton-on-Tees *(Stockton & Hartlepool Branch):* The North Eastern Railway also had a large fleet of 4-6-0 locomotives. There were 103 at the Grouping, which were increased to 135 by the LNER, and they were used on all varieties of freight and passenger workings. No. 840 was the first of Class S3 and was built at Darlington in 1919. It is seen here as LNER Class B16 No. 1400 in September 1947.

97 (below left): The North Eastern Railway 0-8-0 locomotives were particularly intended for mineral train working. They were introduced in 1901 and some were fitted with piston valves (Class T) and some with slide valves (Class T1). One of the piston valve engines was rebuilt with a 5ft. 6in. diameter boiler which was originally built to replace the domeless boilers on the Hull & Barnsley 0-8-0 engines. However, the engines of the Hull & Barnsley Railway had a short life and further use was found for the boilers on the North Eastern Railway's 0-8-0 locomotives. The engine in the picture is No. 2119, but the location is unknown.

100 (below) West Monkseaton *(Blyth & Tyne Branch):* With the housing development in the area, the LNER decided to build a new station between Backworth and Monkseaton, and this was opened on 20th March 1933. At the same time, the electric stock used on the North Tyneside lines was running in a teak finish livery which made the vehicles drab and unattractive.

101 (above right) South Gosforth Car Sheds: In 1938 the electric trains commenced running to South Shields, on the south side of the River Tyne, and the newer North Eastern coaches were reconditioned and painted in the new red and cream livery, similar to that used by the North Eastern Railway, on the first electric train, in 1904.

102 (below right) Jarrow *(Pelaw & South Shields Branch):* Occasionally, steam-hauled trains were to be seen on the electrified routes, such as this set of North Eastern Railway coaches hauled by Class G5 0-4-4T, No. 2098. The headlamp code carried by the engine signified a passenger train between Newcastle and South Shields, and not the standard 'No. 1 braked merchandise train composed of coaching stock, running at an average speed of 40m.p.h. or upwards'!

103 (above): The new stock, introduced by the LNER in 1937, consisted mainly of articulated units and these were generally kept to the North Tyneside lines. This twin set is in the wartime blue and off white livery with the LNER totem, which replaced the red and cream livery from 1941.

105 (below) South Shields *(Pelaw & South Shields Branch):* Railways in the north-east did not suffer severely in World War II, but electric car No. 23249 was damaged beyond repair by a German bomb.

104 (below left): The LNER stock and the modernized NER stock were both fitted with bucket seats as introduced on the tourist train sets in 1933. The seats in one half of the saloon faced one way and in the other half they faced the opposite way, as seen in this view.

106 (above left) Hartlepool *(Ferryhill & Hartlepool Branch):* Many branch lines in the north-east were worked by Sentinel steam railcars, which required only a driver and fireman, and no guard. The first cars supplied to the LNER were of the 2 cylinder variety but as the design was developed, 6 cylinder and 12 cylinder cars appeared. The vertical water tube boiler could lay down a thick and pungent smoke screen if not fired correctly, as No. 225 *True Blue* is doing whilst waiting at Hartlepool. No. 225 was a 2 cylinder car.

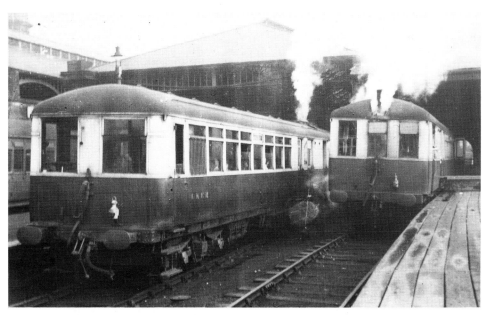

107 (below left) Pickering *(Whitby Branch):* Locomotives using the same boiler and cylinders as the railcars were used for shunting duties, and some were provided with two gear ratios to give shunting and running speeds. No. 81 was one of the double-geared engines, and it was also fitted with vacuum brake equipment to enable it to work passenger trains from Pickering to Scarborough in the event of the failure of the rostered Sentinel railcar.

108 (above) Scarborough *(York & Scarborough Branch):* Two Sentinel railcars, with 12 cylinder No. 220 *Defence* on the left, and an unidentified 6 cylinder car on the right.

109 (below) Scarborough: As summer traffic at Scarborough increased, the station had to be extended at various times and, standing at platform 7, in what was originally the 1845 York & North Midland Railway goods shed, is No. 2236 *British Queen*, the Sentinel car used on the Pickering service. The car appears to have arrived hauling one of the ex-Great Northern Railway 6 wheel coaches which were used at various locations, although some specially-designed 4 wheel trailers were built for use with the railcars.

110 Hull *(Hull & Selby Branch):* 'Foreign' engines often worked in, or into, the north-east, including former Great Northern Railway engines from Doncaster, such as Class K2, 2-6-0 No. 4665, seen at Dairycoates on a fish train.

111 Scarborough *(York & Scarborough Branch):* Scarborough saw engines off the Great Central section during the summer months, such as 'Director' class 4-4-0, No. 5435 *Sir Clement Royds,* in June 1939. It is seen passing Falsgrave signal box, at the entrance to the station.

112 Scarborough: The most impressive Great Central Railway engines to visit the east coast were the Class B7 4-6-0 locomotives, and in this view No. 5475 stands outside Scarborough Shed, awaiting turning for its return working.

113 Cottingham South *(Hull & Scarborough Branch):* The Hull & Barnsley Railway had five 4-4-0 engines, which were built for use on their Hull-Cudworth-Sheffield (Midland) trains, but they ended their days working from Botanic Gardens, one of the North Eastern Railway sheds at Hull. They were usually employed on secondary and local passenger trains.

114 York Layerthorpe *(Derwent Valley Light Railway):* The DVLR passenger service was not a great success and, to save money, the company purchased two Ford buses fitted with rail wheels, which were designed to run back to back with the leading bus hauling the other. The two vehicles became redundant when the passenger service was withdrawn in 1926 and they were sold for use in Ireland.

115 York Layerthorpe *(Derwent Valley Railway):* The DVLR dropped the word 'Light' from its title and, in 1977 introduced a passenger service to Dunnington with the object of attracting railway enthusiasts and families, who were visiting the National Railway Museum, to the line. The inaugural train on 4th May was hauled by 0-6-0T *Joem*, which was built by British Railways in 1951 as a Class J72 engine to a design which first appeared in 1898.

116 Easingwold *(Easingwold Railway):*
This line had to rely on Class J71 and J72 0-6-0T locomotives which were hired from Brtitish Railways when its own engine was beyond repair. In June 1957, the Railway Correspondence & Travel Society organized a tour over the line, from Alne to Easingwold and back, when the hardy passengers were conveyed in open wagons which were specially swept clean for the occasion. The engine was Class J71, No. 68246 from York Shed, which carried a couple of Union flags for the occasion.

117 Pateley Bridge *(Nidd Valley Light Railway):* The passenger service from Pateley Bridge terminated at Lofthouse-in-Nidderdale, although the goods and workmen's trains continued to the reservoirs which were under construction further up the valley. Used on the passenger service was this former Great Western Railway steam railcar, the body of which was discovered, in 1961 in a Leeds scrapyard, 31 years after the passenger service had been withdrawn.

118 Fishponds *(Sand Hutton Railway)*: The North Eastern R.. officials at York were very help. Sir Robert Walker, the owner SHLR, which started life in 191.. 15in. gauge line, with the B.. Lowke built locomotive *Sy.* which was named after Lady W..

119 Warthill *(LNER and SHLR)*:   Following World War I, Sir Robert Walker decided to convert the line to a light railway, to carry passengers and freight. A Light Railway Order became operative on 1st May 1920 and it was intended that the 15in. gauge line would be extended. However, when a quantity of 18in, gauge engines, which were surplus to WD requirements, became available, it was decided to purchase some of these and to change the gauge of the original line, and also parts of the extension which had already been laid. At Warthill, the Light Railway connected with the LNER York to Hull line, and sidings and a ramp were constructed for the interchange of goods traffic. These were arranged so that bulk loads could be transferred from LNER to SHLR wagons, or from SHLR wagons to LNER wagons, with the minimum of effort, the load being handled downwards as this required no lifting, as seen in this view.

120 Claxton Brickworks *(SHLR):*   The line served brickworks at Claxton. Unfortunately Sir Robert Walker died in 1930 at the age of 39 and, with the rapidly decreasing amount of traffic, the line was closed in 1932. A saloon coach from the line, which spent many years as a cricket pavilion, has been restored and now operates on the Lincolnshire Coast Light Railway.

121 Seahouses *(North Sunderland Railway):*   This was another line which had to hire locomotives from the LNER, the choice usually falling on Class Y7 0-4-0T, No. 986, photographed at Seahouses in 1947. This engine, by then renumbered 68089, was still working on the line when it closed in October 1951.

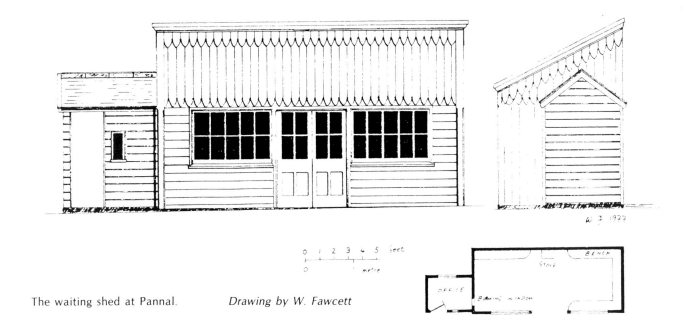

The waiting shed at Pannal.   *Drawing by W. Fawcett*

122 Ryton *(Newcastle & Carlisle Branch):*   A typical LNER train on a major branch at the time of nationalization. The engine is a post-war built Class B1 4-6-0, No. 1219, seen in green livery, hauling Gresley pre-war corridor stock. The location is near Ryton, with a North Eastern Railway slotted post distant signal (with modifications) in the foreground and a standard North Eastern Railway mile post just beyond it. The engine went to Carlisle (Canal) Shed on delivery from the North British Locomotive Co. in August 1947, together with No. 1217, 1221 and 1222, replacing the Class D49 locomotives which were rostered for the Newcastle trains. Each day three engines were required to make two return trips to Newcastle.

British Railways Takes Over

British Railways inherited a railway system which had been badly hit by years of war, when traffic had to be worked by run down engines and life-expired rolling stock. Nevertheless, in the 2½ years after the war ended, the LNER made great efforts to overcome these difficulties. Some people seemed to think that nationalization would cure all the ills, but the legend BRITISH RAILWAYS on the engines did not make the boiler steam any better on the poor coal, or improve the cleanliness of the rolling stock. Many changes took place gradually, just as they did 25 years earlier at the birth of the LNER. The locomotives and coaches appeared in new liveries, with all but former Great Western Railway engines being renumbered to distinguish their ownership, and the whole system was divided into six regions. The LNER was split into three with the North-Eastern Region covering what was latterly the North-Eastern Area of the LNER, and originally the North Eastern Railway. Its headquarters were at York, with some of the chief officers being shared with the Eastern Region, the southern portion of the LNER. Officials with no NER or LNER tradition or experience behind them came and went without making much impact, as the Region struggled on. Bomb-damaged stations were rebuilt, large marshalling yards became the order of the day and, at long last, the York re-signalling scheme was commissioned, having been commenced prior to World War II.

Branch line traffic tended to decrease, although petrol rationing, and the shortage of new cars, kept passenger figures high for a time on some branches. The introduction of the first diesel railcars in 1954, unattractive in shape and livery, meant that, at last, branch services could be improved and greater economies made. These new railcars led to the withdrawal of many of the tank engines which had worked the branch lines for years. Unfortunately, many of the short distance railcars were used on long distance services, which did not help to retain passengers, and there were repeated complaints about their heating systems and their general noisiness. However, there is no doubt that the railcars prolonged the life of many branch lines.

Branch line closures started again in April 1950 with the withdrawal of the Bedlington to Morpeth service followed by Seamer to Pickering, Malton to Driffield, and Knaresborough to Pilmoor. In 1951, the Garforth to Castleford branch and the Pateley Bridge and Waterhouses branches disappeared from the timetable, followed, in 1952, by Ferryhill to Spennymoor, Ferryhill to Stockton, Sunderland to West Hartlepool (via Wellfield), Ferryhill to West Hartlepool, and Kirkby Stephen to Tebay.

Dr Richard Beeching was appointed as the new Chairman of British Railways from 1st June 1961 at a salary of £24,000 a year and, on 27th March 1963, he announced his famous plan for improving the railway system. This included suggestions for closing 2,363 passenger stations and eliminating the stopping passenger train. The publication of the plan led to much hostility, with newspaper headlines such as 'Ramblers will fight rail closures', 'MP fights for Whitby Station', 'Railway closure could leave people stranded', 'UDC to fight against rail line closure', 'Tourist trade will be badly affected' and 'Beeching 500 per cent out says pamphlet' etc. Nevertheless, most of the proposed cuts did go through, some after lengthy public enquiries, until the north-east was virtually denuded of branch lines, although some were reprieved, such as the Middlesbrough to Whitby branch, or delayed, such as the Haltwhistle to Alston line, because of unsuitable roads.

On branches that did not close, intermediate stations were closed and many that remained open were unstaffed for part or all of the day, with 'paytrains' on some branches. This opened the way for vandalism and neglect, with stations becoming so disreputable that passengers found other ways of travelling. At the time of writing, the railway system is grinding to a halt for three days a week, driving away more passengers, and already warning headlines are appearing. Only this morning a Member of Parliament is reported as saying 'Seaside line could be killed', referring to the York to Scarborough branch, which is already heavily subsidized.

Many of our early railways were built when both road and rail traffic was light and when level crossings caused little inconvenience. Later, the Act of Parliament for the construction of a line stated that where road and rail crossed, a bridge should be provided, but it has not been possible to implement this retrospectively and thus many early lines, with level crossings and no bridges, are the same today, especially in areas where the land is flat and contours cannot be used. Thus the York to Scarborough line, with a manned level crossing at almost every intermediate station, or where the station used to be, and with numerous minor crossings in addition, costs a fortune just to man the signal boxes for two shifts a day on six days a week, plus Sunday duty at time and three-quarters overtime. What a pity that the Central Train Control, which was authorized for the York to Beverley branch, was not transferred to the York to Scarborough line when the former closed without the apparatus being used.

In addition to the York to Scarborough line, the future must be bleak, indeed, for the Hull to Scarborough branch, which has been threatened with closure for years, and the Middlesbrough to Whitby service. The Darlington to Bishop Auckland service continues as the truncated remains of the Darlington-Bishop Auckland-Crook-Tow Law-Blackhill branch, and on Tyneside, the Metro system is gradually taking over North Eastern Railway branches which were once alive with passengers.

Where will it end? No one knows, but this work is an attempt to show what the branches were like when the railway was the main form of transport.

123 Market Weighton *(York & Market Weighton Branch):* When British Railways was formed on 1st January 1948, few visible changes took place immediately, but gradually new liveries were introduced, including Regional colours. That chosen for the North Eastern Region was tangerine and, as station signs were repainted, they appeared in the new colour. Even the covers of the public timetables were coloured tangerine. In this view, taken at Market Weighton, 'the crossroads of the Yorkshire Wolds', the footbridge and right of way notices, together with the signal box nameboard, have just been repainted in the new livery, and this photograph is one of a series taken to record the occasion.

124 Kippax *(Leeds & Castleford Branch):* Little photographed were the stations on the Garforth to Castleford branch, with their typical North Eastern Railway architecture of around 1880. In fact, Kippax was opened in August 1878 and closed to passengers in 1951.

125 Market Weighton: At the front of the station there were no signs of ownership and, in fact, no indication that the building was a railway station. Externally, the building had changed little in its century of existence. If it wasn't for the cars, the concrete urn, and the wooden refreshment room it would be virtually impossible to date the photograph. It was actually photographed in 1948, in the early day of British Railways. The station closed in 1965 and it has been replaced by a small housing estate.

126 Bowers Halt *(Leeds & Castleford Branch):* This small station was opened in December 1934 to serve the nearby Allerton Main colliery, as proclaimed on the signal box. The word 'Halt' was dropped from the title in 1937. The NER pattern water crane in the foreground, with the large diameter balance weight, is of particular interest.

127 East Boldon *(Pelaw & Sunderland Branch):*   Although there were schemes to electrify the South Shields to Sunderland, and Pelaw to Sunderland lines, electrification never reached Sunderland. Consequently, the local services continued to be worked by steam and notably by the Class G5 0-4-4T engines, such as No. 67310, seen running bunker first on a 3 coach push and pull set forming the 1.12p.m. Sunderland to South Shields train. This view was taken on a cold day in January 1954.

128 Cox Green *(Penshaw Branch):* Durham Shed had a small stud of Class G5 engines for local services, and this view shows No. 67258 with the 1.42p.m. Durham to Sunderland train in March 1957. A total of 110 Class G5 engines were built by the NER between 1894 and 1901 and they were used on branch line services throughout the system, until displaced by diesel multiple units in the 1950s. This led to their rapid disappearance and they were all withdrawn by the end of 1958.

129 (below) Yarm *(Leeds Northern Branch):* The Stockton & Darlington Railway opened a coal depot at Yarm in October 1825, only a couple of weeks after the opening of the world's first steam-worked public railway. A horse-drawn passenger service was introduced later but this short branch never had a steam-worked passenger service. The Leeds Northern Railway passed under the Stockton & Darlington line when it extended to Stockton in 1852, and in 1871 the S&D depot was closed and the coal traffic was transferred to the Leeds Northern station which was only a few hundred yards away. In this view, Class G5 No. 67349 is seen with a Northallerton-bound train at the ex-Leeds Northern station at Yarm. The tunnel under the Darlington to Yarm road, and under the former Stockton & Darlington branch to Yarm, can be seen in the far distance.

130 (above right) Alston *(Alston Branch):* One of the most photographed stations in the north-east in recent years was Alston, at the end of the branch from Haltwhistle. This single platform station dated from 1852, although, over the years, the train shed roof was altered. The Class G5 engine appearing in many photographs was No. 67315, the Alston engine, but in this 1953 view the engine is No. 67265, a temporary replacement from Hexham Shed.

131 (below right) Harrogate *(Leeds Northern Branch):* Another Class G5 engine which usually kept to its own branch was the Pateley Bridge engine, No. 67253. This last day view, taken on 31st January 1951, marks the end of the passenger service, with extra passengers aboard to mark this sad occasion.

134 (below) Filey *(Hull & Scarborough Branch):* The north end of Filey Station with Class D49 No. 62747 *The Percy* arriving on a train from Scarborough to Hull. The goods yard was entered by a separate road crossing with its own gates, with the warehouse, seen in the background, behind the upper quadrant signal.

132 (above left) Leeds City *(Leeds & Selby Branch):* The Class D20 4-4-0 locomotives were, at one time, the top passenger engines on the North Eastern Railway but, in the 1950s, they were to be found on branch workings, such as in this view of No. 62341 arriving at Leeds from Selby. The photograph was taken by the late H. Gelder of Leeds, a lifelong railway enthusiast, who died after the derailment of a York to Liverpool train at Ulleskelf, in December 1981, as he was returning home after a railway outing.

133 (below left) Gilling *(Thirsk & Malton Branch):* The Class D49 engines, which first appeared from Darlington Works in 1927, were also downgraded to minor branch lines. This view shows No. 62726 *The Meynell* with a Pickering to York train.

135 (left) Seaton Bank *(Stockton & Sunderland Branch):* Handling unfitted loaded mineral trains down the banks in the north-east required skill and local knowledge which was obtainable only from years of experience on the footplate. Here No. 65894 descends Seaton Bank, and the gradient post indicates a fall at 1 in 45, steepening to 1 in 42. This Class J27 0-6-0, the last of the class to be built, was one of the five withdrawn on 9th September 1967, marking the end of steam on British Railways in the north-east. However, it was purchased by the North Eastern Locomotive Preservation Group and is now to be found on the North York Moors Railway, based at Grosmont Shed.

136 (above) Ushaw Moor *(Dearness Valley Branch):* The final 0-6-0 engines built at Darlington Works were of Class J39, which was designed by H. N. Gresley. With 5ft. 2in. wheels, and automatic brakes, they were used on a variety of tasks, such as goods and mineral trains during the week and excursions at the weekends. The location here is of interest as No. 64927 crosses one of the last wooden viaducts in use on BR in North-East England. However, this was not a particularly old structure as it had been renewed in 1896 at a cost of £2,220 6s 9d by the contractor J. Scott. Most NER wooden viaducts were replaced in stone, brick or metal between 1865 and 1875.

139 (above) Ruswarp *(Whitby Branch)*: This bridge across the River Esk, situated just west of the station, had a very convenient footpath running alongside the tracks, from which Class Q6 0-8-0 No. 63398 was photographed in 1960, when returning to Middlesbrough on the Whitby pick-up goods. When opened by the Whitby & Pickering Railway in 1835, the bridge was built of timber.

140 (below) Coxhoe Junction *(Bishop Auckland & Ferryhill Branch)*: At one time, the signal box at Coxhoe Junction controlled the East Coast Main Line seen in the foreground, the 'old main line' via Leamside passing below the box, the Coxhoe (WH) branch diverging off the Leamside line under the bridge, the Spennymoor and Bishop Auckland line crossing on the overbridge, and the Hartlepool line up Kelloe Bank, diverging from the Bishop Auckland line on the embankment. Traces of the old curve to the Bishop Auckland line can be seen in the right foreground but this was superseded by the overbridge. The box and the bridge have now been demolished.

37 (above left) Enthorpe Bank *(Market Weighton & Driffield Branch)*: Constructed by the Scarborough, Bridlington & West Riding Junction Railway, this line was opened in 1890 and it became a useful route for trains to the east coast during the busy summer months. Favourites on many of these trains were the Class B16 4-6-0 engines which were designed by Vincent Raven, with three cylinders and 5ft. 8in. wheels. This is Selby-allocated locomotive No. 61433 on the 9.05a.m. (SO) Liverpool (Exchange) to Scarborough (Londesborough Road), identifiable by the tablet number (C239) carried on the top lamp bracket. It is seen hard at work tackling the long 1 in 95 climb to Enthorpe.

38 (below left) Enthorpe Bank: The same engine No. 61433, is seen at the top of the bank, where the line passes through a cutting in the Wolds' chalk. On this occasion the train is the 9.35a.m. (SO) Sowerby Bridge to Scarborough. On both occasions, No. 61433 would have taken over from a London Midland Region engine at Gascoigne Wood, which would be reached by running light engine from its home depot at Selby.

141 Whitby *(Whitby Branch):* In its final days, the long-established Malton to Whitby pick-up goods was worked by a York-based engine and Class B1 4-6-0 No. 61319 was on this turn on 24th August 1964, seen here ready to leave for Malton. The former engine shed, which was closed in 1959, can be seen in the background.

142 Biddick Lane *(Pontop & South Shields Branch):* The iron-ore trains between Tyne Dock and Consett were a favourite subject for photographers as the Class 9F 2-10-0 engines blasted their way up the steep gradients. However, their photogenic appeal declined with the introduction of diesel locomotives.

143 Wapping Bridge *(Newcastle, Leamside & Ferryhill Branch):* The small signal box at Wapping Bridge, which was situated a mile north of Fencehouses, was at the southern end of the four track section from Penshaw North. At this point it was usual to find one or more freight trains waiting to follow a passenger train to Leamside. In this view, photographed in June 1963, Class K1 2-6-0 No. 62028, with a ballast train, is getting a clear run on the passenger lines, with no train waiting on the goods lines.

144 Penshaw North *(Newcastle, Leamside & Ferryhill Branch):*   The box at Penshaw North controlled the junction between the line to Sunderland, seen below the centre of the girders, and the line to Washington, on the extreme left. The Tyne Dock Class 9F locomotive is taking the line which crosses Victoria Bridge and which spans the River Wear, to Washington, where the engine will run round its train and set off for Consett with a load of small coal. A brake van at each end of the train saved shunting movements at Washington. The engine is fitted with Westinghouse pumps for opening the wagon doors for easy discharging at Consett, but this train consists of normal hopper wagons, which are unbraked, and fitted with bottom doors.

145 Haltwhistle *(Newcastle & Carlisle Branch):* On 11th December 1955, Class 3MT 2-6-0 No. 77011 was transferred to Alston to work the branch service to and from Haltwhistle, where connection was made with Newcastle to Carlisle trains. However, on 30th March 1957, No. 77014 of the same class was on the branch train, and is seen standing at the island platform at Haltwhistle, with the River South Tyne on the left.

146 Prudhoe (*Newcastle & Carlisle Branch*): Diesel railcars displaced the useful Class G5 0-4-4T engines which, for many years, had worked the Newcastle to Hexham service, and this Metro-Cammell unit is seen leaving Prudhoe, with the River Tyne in the background.

147 Willington Quay (*Riverside Branch*): The last regular passenger train ran on this once-electrified branch on 20th July 1973, and it comprised a 4 car set forming the 16.40 from Newcastle.

148 West Auckland *(Barnard Castle & Bishop Auckland Branch):* A view of this unusual station seen from a different angle than that shown in *Plate 71* again showing the platforms facing the same direction. The train is the 16.15 from Bishop Auckland on 27th February 1962 and the line was closed later in the same year.

149 Crimple Viaduct *(Church Fenton & Harrogate Branch):* The Leeds & Thirsk Railway served Harrogate with a station at Starbeck, but the York & North Midland line from Church Fenton and Wetherby ran nearer to the centre of Harrogate by bridging the Crimple Valley on this fine viaduct of 31 arches. The viaduct also crossed the Leeds & Thirsk line which ran along the valley to Starbeck. In 1862, a connection was built between the two lines to enable trains from both Leeds and Church Fenton to use the new station at Harrogate.

151 (right) Wylam Scars *(Newcastle & Carlisle Branch):* On the following day, Class 47, No 1104 was on a similar working and is between Prudhoe and Wylam, running along the south bank of the Tyne. This same site was chosen by the artist J. W. Carmichael, 136 years earlier, for one of his 'Views on the Newcastle & Carlisle Railway' which was published in 1836.

150 (above) Blaydon *(Newcastle & Carlisle Branch):* This scene was photographed by Ian S. Carr, who has, for many years, specialized in capturing trains in the north-east which have been diverted from their correct route, usually because of engineering works or mishaps. On this occasion, No. 9002 *The King's Own Yorkshire Light Infantry* comes to a stand at Blaydon on 23rd July 1972. The train was the 11.00 Edinburgh to King's Cross which had been retimed to depart at 10.00 because of the longer journey involved by travelling via Carlisle and Hexham, caused by engineering works at Dunbar. The train, in fact, was held at Blaydon for almost an hour because of fire breaking out on a locomotive at Scotswood.

Some Goods and Mineral Lines in the North-East

152 (above left) Ryhope Colliery Junction *(Sunderland & Castle Eden Branch):* A train, headed by No. 9005 *The Prince of Wales's Own Regiment of Yorkshire* is seen heading south from Sunderland on the route of the old Londonderry Railway, which was purchased by the NER in 1900. A new link line from Seaham to Hart provided a coastal route without the gradients of the Castle Eden line and, eventually, all passenger trains between Sunderland, Hartlepool and Stockton used the new route. The abandoned lines from Ryhope and Silksworth collieries trail in on the left to join what was originally the Durham & Sunderland Railway down Seaton Bank from Murton. At Ryhope, at the foot of the bank, all passenger trains heading for Sunderland had to stop to ensure that they were under the full control of the driver. This followed an accident to a Liverpool to Newcastle express which got out of control and was derailed.

153 (below left) Ryhope Colliery: The line to serve Ryhope and Silksworth collieries was not a true NER branch as it was originally built by the colliery companies to get their coal to the Londonderry Railway for transportation to Sunderland. However, the branch was worked by the NER and its successors using 0-6-0 engines, such as Class J27 No. 65872, seen in this view in 1966.

154 Silksworth Colliery: Class J27 No. 65894 shunts the colliery sidings at Silksworth on 8th September 1967, the day before the locomotive was withdrawn from service. It had been specially cleaned for the occasion by local enthusiasts.

155 (above) Bishopton Lane *(Simpasture Branch):* This line, between Stillington North Junction and Simpasture Junction, south of Shildon, was built by the Clarence Railway and was opened in 1833, but its only use for regular passenger traffic appears to have been between November 1841 and February 1842 when the Stockton & Darlington Railway ran a short-lived service between Darlington and Coxhoe. Originally, the line carried coal to Port Clarence, on the north bank of the River Tees, but, after the opening of the line from Carlton to Bowesfield Junction in 1877, the flow of traffic tended to be towards the south bank of the Tees at Middlesbrough.

156 Elstob Lane *(Simpasture Branch):* By using the Simpasture branch and the line to Bowesfield Junction, the coal traffic could avoid passing through Darlington and also the use of the crossing on the level of the East Coast Main Line. As most of the Simpasture branch carried only mineral traffic, it was decided to electrify it by the overhead system and this was brought into use in 1915, although it was abandoned in 1935. This is one of ten electric locomotives, and is seen hauling a train load of empty wagons back to Shildon.

157 Gateshead *(Redheugh Deviation Branch):* When the Newcastle to Dunston service ceased in 1926 the line, which was built to replace the Redheugh Incline, reverted to freight traffic use only. This line was from King Edward Bridge Junction, Gateshead, dropping down on the east side of the main line before passing below it to join the line from Low Fell at Norwood Junction. British Rail has now diverted Newcastle to Carlisle trains over this route, bringing passenger traffic back to the line.

158 Belmont Junction *(Newcastle, Leamside & Ferryhill Branch):* The Newcastle & Darlington Junction Railway's terminus at Gilesgate, Durham, was at the end of a short branch off the 'old main line' at Belmont Junction. Gilesgate was opened in 1844, but it closed to passengers in 1857 when a new Durham Station was opened on the branch from Leamside to Bishop Auckland. This view was taken from the top of the old water tank at Belmont Junction and shows Class 17 'Clayton' No. D8598 entering the branch in August 1966, three months before Gilesgate Goods Station closed.

159 Monkseaton *(Tynemouth Branch):*   A 1952 view of this spacious station, which, in 1915, replaced an earlier station known as Whitley until 1882.

160 Monkseaton: The old station at Monkseaton which was replaced by the one pictured above.

161 Benton *(Blyth & Tyne Branch):* The electrified route through South Gosforth ran on the west side of the East Coast Main Line and thus had to cross it to reach the coast. In this view, a train bound for Monkseaton crosses the main line, which disappears into the distance to Forest Hall.

162 Benton: A train from the coast is about to cross the bridge over the main line *(see above).* The LNER 1937 stock is in the BR green livery.

163 Trafalgar Yard (*Quayside Branch*):   In conjunction with the electrification of the line from Newcastle to Tynemouth in 1904, the North Eastern Railway electrified the steeply-graded branch down to the quayside at Newcastle. Much of the line was in tunnels and it proved to be a difficult line to operate with steam locomotives as they worked hard up the bank. Electrification made a big improvement in the working conditions for the footplate crews. A third rail pick-up was used in the tunnels, but because of the danger to shunters, overhead pick-up was used in the yards which were situated at the top and bottom. Two electric locomotives were built for working the line but they were replaced by diesels in 1964. However, the line continued in use for only another five years as it closed in June 1969. Fortunately, one of the electric locomotives has been preserved and can be seen, in the full glory of its restored North Eastern livery, in the National Railway Museum at York.

Engine Sheds

Many of the country branch line sheds accommodated only one engine, whilst those on the major branches could be of considerable size, with the largest straight sheds, at Scarborough and Stockton, each having eight dead end roads. The largest depot in the north-east was actually on a branch, rather than on the main line, and this was Hull (Dairycoates), with six adjoining roundhouses and two straight sheds.

Most branches were worked by engines from the sheds at each end. At one end was the shed at, or near, the junction with the main line or major branch, and at the other end, the small shed was at the terminus. The shed at the terminus, with one engine, usually had a staff of five, with a driver and fireman to work the early turn and another crew to work the late shift, changing over weekly. The fifth man was responsible for lighting up the engine each morning, and for keeping it clean. He was normally a footplateman who could relieve if one of the other men failed to turn up for duty due to illness etc. To cover the annual leave of the footplatemen, it was usual to send out a spare man from the parent shed, and he was expected to lodge for the week as he would be employed either on the first train out or the last train in. However, some men preferred to cycle out to the branch shed in time to work the first train out, perform their turn of duty, and then return home by train with their bicycle, or go out by train, and cycle home after working the last train. Others would sleep in the shed and get a morning's casual labour on a nearby farm before going on duty, thus earning a few extra shillings.

Most of the branch line termini had a locomotive turntable and watering facilities, but coal was taken at the parent shed during the day. The regular boiler washout had to be carried out at the parent shed and this usually took place during a 24 hour period, with the crew exchanging the branch engine for one of a similar type, collecting their own engine 24 hours later after the boiler had been washed out and the fire had been re-lit. Similar coverage, but for longer spells, was arranged to cover minor and major repairs.

Although Sentinel steam railcars worked on many branches, they were not usually stationed at sheds where there was no locomotive. Presumably, this was because there was no emergency cover if the railcar proved unserviceable first thing in the morning, dislocating the life of the dale, with passengers being unable to get to work or school. Consequently, sheds such as Pateley Bridge, Masham, Wearhead, Middleton-in-Teesdale, Alston and Richmond were usually provided with a Class G5 0-4-4T or a Class J21 0-6-0 locomotive, which had to have something seriously wrong with them to stop them working the first train. However, with the introduction of diesel railcars, this practice was abandoned and if the engines would not start after a cold night, then it was hard luck! In this case, the first train ran very late or was cancelled altogether.

The closure of branches has inevitably meant the closure of sheds. Some of the larger sheds, notably Hull Botanic Gardens and Thornaby, have survived but others the size of Scarborough and Stockton have vanished, together with Hull Dairycoates. The small branch line shed with one engine has gone forever but, fortunately, has been captured on film by intrepid enthusiasts venturing into the wilds of upper Weardale or the heights of Alston.

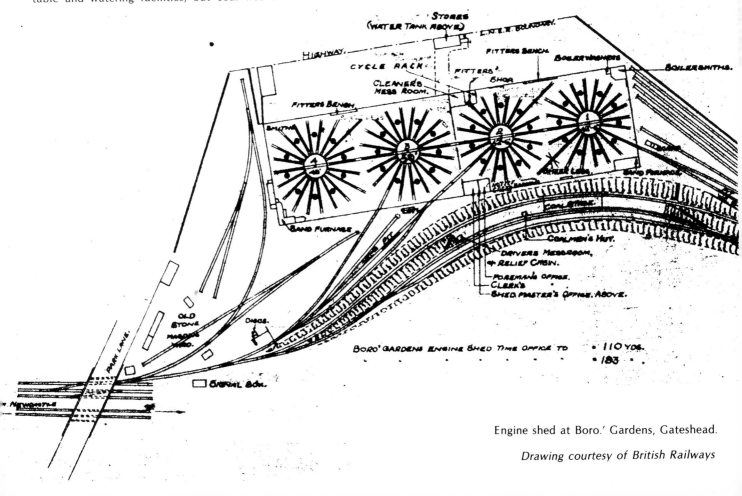

Engine shed at Boro.' Gardens, Gateshead.

Drawing courtesy of British Railways

164 Masham *(Masham Branch):* This small wooden shed could be entered only by using the turntable, which was unusual for a North Eastern Railway shed. In LNER days, the Masham engine was usually Class G5 0-4-4T No. 1911, but when the branch passenger service was withdrawn, on 1st January 1931, No. 1911 was moved to Leeds (Neville Hill) Shed.

165 Pateley Bridge *(Pateley Bridge Branch):* Another wooden shed which, in this case, replaced an earlier stone structure. The usual occupant was Class G5 No. 1839, later renumbered 67253, which remained at Pateley Bridge until the shed closed on 1st April 1951.

166 Pelton Level *(Pontop & South Shields Branch):* This shed was on a locomotive-worked section of line between the top of one rope-worked incline and the foot of another, on the old Stanhope & Tyne route. The engine in the shed is Class J73 0-6-0T No. 549, which moved to Hull in 1937, although the shed continued in use until the 1960s.

167 Wearhead *(Wear Valley Branch):* This brick-built shed was opened when the branch was extended from Stanhope in 1895. The Class J21 0-6-0, No. 1566, was stationed at Wearhead during the summer of 1935 and, in October of that year, it was replaced by No. 314 of the same class, which remained at Wearhead until the shed closed in June 1953.

168 Barnard Castle *(Darlington & Barnard Castle Branch):* This two road shed was built in two parts. One section was authorized in 1864, and was presumably completed in 1865, and the other half was authorized in January 1875, and may have been completed in that year. In 1923, the shed accommodated seven engines, but at the time of closure, in 1937, the only engine remaining was Class E4 2-4-0 No. 7463.

169 Waskerley *(Pontop & Sou*
Shields Branch): There were tw
shed buildings at Waskerley and th
second shed can be seen in th
distance on the left. Usually, eigh
or nine engines were based at th
remote depot. It was closed i
September 1940 and little trace
the building remains, although th
coal stage can be easily discerned

170 Bowes Bridge *(Tanfield Branch):* This building appears to have started life as the engine house or boiler house for a winding engine. There is a chimney on the left-hand side which is clearly visible. The two engines in this view are both 0-6-2 tanks, being Class N9 No. 1643 and Class N10 No. 1138.

171 Bowes Bridge: In December 1942, or January 1943, the shed at Bowes Bridge was destroyed by fire and for twelve years the two engines stood each night in the roofless remains of the shed. However, a new shed was eventually built and it was in use until September 1962. Four years later it was demolished and the rubble was used to fill the turntable pit. It can be seen that the chimney mentioned and partly pictured in *Plate 170* has been demolished although the base remains.

172 Brotherton Tubular Bridge *(Knottingley Branch):* The York and North Midland Railway's main line from York to Normanton was opened in 1840, giving a route to London (Euston Square), but later the Company saw the possibility of reaching London via the East Coast route. This was achieved by building a branch from Burton Salmon to Knottingley to join the Lancashire & Yorkshire Railway, and then by using the latter company's route, to join the Great Northern Railway north of Doncaster. Near Ferrybridge, the branch had to cross the River Aire and for this task, Robert Stephenson designed a twin tubular bridge. Goods traffic commenced running over a temporary bridge in April 1850 and in July 1851 permission was given to open the first tube to passenger traffic. When in October 1851, notice was given that the second tube was ready, the Board of Trade Inspecting Officer found that both tubes were unsatisfactory as the sides sloped inwards from bottom to top giving limited clearance for trains. Some delay was caused as Robert Stephenson was abroad but when he returned, a year later, he suggested that the sides of the tubes be made vertical to gain the required clearance. To allow for the increased width at the top of each tube, a piece of boiler plate 21½in. wide was inserted. This cured the problem, and from 11th October 1852, both tubes were available for traffic. As the railway crossed the river on the skew, the 237ft. long tubes were staggered by some 25ft. In 1900 a tender for the replacement of the two tubes was awarded to the Cleveland Bridge & Engineering Co. Ltd., at a price of £17,700 and the new bridge was built using the original abutments.

173 Victoria Bridge *(Newcastle, Leamside & Ferryhill Branch):* This fine bridge, across the River Wear, was erected by the small Durham Junction Railway and, at one time, carried the East Coast Main Line between Darlington and Gateshead. The structure received its name as it was completed on the Coronation Day of the young Queen Victoria on 24th June 1838. The bridge took just over two years to build and it consists of four main arches of varying spans between 100ft. and 160ft., and six small arches, with a total length of 811ft. At one end, the bridge crossed old mine workings which had been abandoned in the 18th century and had become flooded, but, in 1859, work started on pumping out the water. Contemporary reports suggest that this was probably an attempt to blackmail the North Eastern Railway by the new owner, who hoped that the Company would pay him to cease his operations to safeguard the safety of the bridge. In common with other notable bridges in the north-east, a commemorative plaque marking the construction of the bridge and the engineers responsible, was, in 1934, affixed to the wall of one of the refuges.

174 Wetheral Viaduct *(Newcastle & Carlisle Branch):* In its sixty miles the Newcastle & Carlisle Railway built some fine viaducts, the most notable being that over the River Eden immediately east of Wetheral Station. This has five semi-circular arches of 80ft. span, with a total length of 564ft. The height above the river is 95ft. The bridge was completed in August 1834 but was not opened to passenger traffic until July 1836.

175 Tees Viaduct *(South Durham & Lancashire Union Branch):* Some of the most striking bridges were on the Stainmore line, between Barnard Castle and Tebay. This is Tees Viaduct, near Barnard Castle, with five 60ft. and two 21ft. spans and a total length of 732ft. Like most of the bridges on the line it has now been dismantled.

176 (right) Wetheral Viaduct: A footpath runs along the north side of Wetheral Viaduct, from Wetheral Station to Corby Gates, giving extensive views along the Eden Valley.

L N E R

NOTICE

PERSONS MUST NOT
RIDE CYCLES OVER
THIS BRIDGE.
BY ORDER

WETHERAL.

177 Lands Viaduct *(Bishop Auckland & Barnard Castle Branch):* In 1863, the South Durham & Lancashire Union Railway opened this single line viaduct across the Gaunless Valley but, fortunately, provided piers wide enough for two tracks. Authority to double the line was given in September 1899, but it was found that, in addition to requiring new girders, the old ones would have to be replaced. Thus it was October 1904 before a tender was accepted for the new steelwork, at a price of £9,858.

178 Lands Viaduct: The line over th viaduct closed in June 1962, followed b the demolition of the girders, but the pier were left as a gaunt reminder of the par the railways had played in the area The line below the viaduct, along th Gaunless Valley, was the Haggerlease (later Butterknowle) branch, opened i 1830 and closed in 1963, which serve numerous small collieries.

Signal Boxes

North Eastern signal boxes came in all shapes and sizes, some with only a handful of levers, and others with hundreds of levers requiring two or three men to operate them. The standard North Eastern Railway method of displaying the box name was by an enamelled sign on the front, but the LNER changed all these to two boards, one at each end of the box, with the letters screwed on to form the name. Boxes came in brick, stone, wood or a combination of two of these materials, varying in length depending on the number of levers, and many boxes show signs of having been extended, as sidings and running lines increased. Boxes also differed between Divisions and the Southern, Central, and Northern Divisions all had designs peculiar to the area concerned.

The waiting shed at Bowes. *Drawing by W. Fawcett*

179 Newton Kyme *(Church Fenton & Harrogate Branch):* A medium-sized box in North Eastern Railway days, with the local staff posing for a picture.

180 Seamer East *(York & Scarborough Branch):* This view of two boxes illustrates the change in design over the years. Only at very few locations were the old boxes allowed to remain, where a use could be found for them as platelayers' stores etc. Another pair of boxes remained for a long time at Burton Salmon, being situated one on each side of the running lines.

181 Cloughton *(Scarborough & Whitby Branch):* Where small boxes were built on station platforms, they were often built below the usual height, as at Cloughton.

182 Arram *(Hull & Scarborough Branch):*   Arram appears to have started life the same size as Cloughton but has had an additional section built on to the right-hand end.

183 Warcop *(Eden Valley Branch):*   Another platform box, of totally different design.

184 Bishop Auckland North *(Durham & Bishop Auckland Branch):* Tall boxes were built where there were sighting difficulties, and this box also has an overhang.

185 Billingham *(Stockton & Hartlepool Branch):* This box not only controls a level crossing, but also provides advertising space!

186 Norton-on-Tees *(Stockton & Hartlepool Branch):* The next box to Billingham, also controlling a level crossing.

187 Penshaw *(Newcastle, Leamside & Ferryhill):* This was a box which was adjacent to the island platform station.

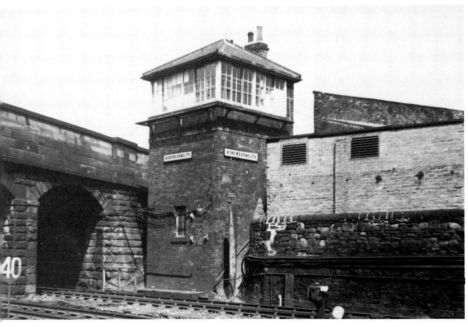

188 Monkwearmouth *(Pelaw & Sunderland Branch):* As it would have been pointless putting a nameboard on the side facing the road bridge at Monkwearmouth, it was placed on the front of the box.

189 Bishop Middleham *(Ferryhill & Stockton Branch):* A box which was open for only one shift a day, as long ago as 1922.

190 Mainsforth Crossing *(Stockton & Hartlepool Branch)*: Many boxes in the north-east were renewed by British Railways, such as Mainsforth Crossing at West Hartlepool (now Hartlepool).

191 Mainsforth Crossing: The new box.

192 Hessle *(Hull & Selby Branch)*: A fine example of a North Eastern Railway brick and wood box. The same design was used for a time in LNER days.

193 Rillington *(York & Scarborough Branch):* This box, situated at the east end of the station, controlled the junction with the Whitby line and a separate gate box was required at the other end of the station to look after the level crossing. When the new box was built in 1959, it was placed at the west end of the station to perform both operations, although the Whitby branch has since disappeared.

194 Rillington: The new box.

195 Low Gates *(Leeds Northern Branch):* On its way to Stockton the Leeds Northern line crossed the main road through Northallerton at the north end of the town, with this box controlling a busy level crossing.

196 Blue Bell *(Blyth & Tyne Old Main Line Branch):* An overhanging box controlling mineral and goods lines, near Backworth.

197 Blue Bell: A British Rail replacement box, using the old base.

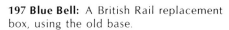

198 Wellfield *(Stockton & Sunderland Branch):* This box controlled the junction between the Bowesfield and Hartlepool lines at the other end of the station, where the earlier box was situated.

199 Knaresborough *(York & Harrogate Branch)*: This box was an oddity, even amongst North Eastern signal boxes!

200 Scarborough *(York & Scarborough Branch)*: Some boxes were of all wood construction, such as the station box at Scarborough.

201 Green Lane *(Pontop & South Shields Branch)*: Boxes mounted on girders over one or more tracks were popular in the Northern Division, with the operating cabin built of wood and prone to catching fire. Many of these boxes, including Green Lane box, therefore, have had their cabins replaced.

202: Before stations were demolished, they were often allowed to deteriorate after damage from vandalism and pure neglect. This is Wetherby in 1968, which has since been demolished.

The End

203: The last piece of line to Wetherby being removed at Church Fenton in 1967. A scene familiar throughout the north-east as branch lines were removed, leaving only photographs and memories to record their passing.

Index

Acknowledgements

P. B. Booth	Plates 124, 126, 155, 181, 184
W. A. Camwell	Plates 75, 77, 79, 133, 164-171
Ian S. Carr	Plates 128, 135, 142-5, 147, 148, 150-4, 158, 162, 173,
C. J. Dean Collection	Plate 160
R. F. Dean	Plate 203
H. Gelder	Plate 132
W. B. Greenfield	Plates 102, 111, 112
T. G. Hepburn	Plates 83, 129
K. Hoole	Plates 115, 140, 161, 178, 202
K. Hoole Collection	35, 40, 41, 57, 60, 62, 65-74, 76, 78, 80, 81, 82, 84-8, 94, 95, 97, 100, 106, 107, 108, 110, 113, 114, 117, 118, 121, 131, 139, 175, 179, 199, 201
H. G. W. Household	Plates 89, 119, 120
G. R. Ives	Plate 136
Lens of Sutton	Plates 16-28, 31-4, 36-9, 42-56, 58, 59, 61, 63, 64
J. F. Mallon	Plate 157
C. Myton	Plates 182, 183, 185-198, 200
North Eastern Railway Association	Plate 29
C. Ord	Plates 116, 137, 138
R. B. Parr	Plate 130
W. Rogerson	Plates 93, 96, 156
T. E. Rounthwaite	Plates 92, 98, 99
J. F. Sedgwick	Plate 134
K. L. Taylor Collection	Plates 1-15, 30
S. E. Teasdale	Plate 127
L. Ward	Plate 180
B. Webb	Plate 141
British Rail	Plates 90, 91, 101, 103, 104, 105, 109, 122, 123, 125, 146, 149, 159, 163, 172, 174, 176, 177